Google® Gmail and Calendar FOR LAWYERS

CAROLE A. LEVITT AND MARK E. ROSCH

Commitment to Quality: The Law Practice Management Section is committed to quality in our publications. Our authors are experienced practitioners in their fields. Prior to publication, the contents of all our books are rigorously reviewed by experts to ensure the highest quality product and presentation. Because we are committed to serving our readers' needs, we welcome your feedback on how we can improve future editions of this book.

Cover design by RIPE Creative, Inc.

Nothing contained in this book is to be considered as the rendering of legal advice for specific cases, and readers are responsible for obtaining such advice from their own legal counsel. This book and any forms and agreements herein are intended for educational and informational purposes only.

The products and services mentioned in this publication are under or may be under trademark or service mark protection. Product and service names and terms are used throughout only in an editorial fashion, to the benefit of the product manufacturer or service provider, with no intention of infringement. Use of a product or service name or term in this publication should not be regarded as affecting the validity of any trademark or service mark.

The Law Practice Management Section, American Bar Association, offers an educational program for lawyers in practice. Books and other materials are published in furtherance of that program. Authors and editors of publications may express their own legal interpretations and opinions, which are not necessarily those of either the American Bar Association or the Law Practice Management Section unless adopted pursuant to the bylaws of the Association. The opinions expressed do not reflect in any way a position of the Section or the American Bar Association.

© 2013 American Bar Association. All rights reserved.

Printed in the United States of America.

16 15 14 13   4 3 2 1

Library of Congress Cataloging-in-Publication Data

Levitt, Carole A.
  Google gmail and calendar in one hour for lawyers / Carole A. Levitt, Mark E. Rosch.
    pages cm
  Includes index.
  ISBN 978-1-61438-727-5
  1. Law offices—United States—Automation. 2. Electronic mail systems—Management—
United States. I. Rosch, Mark E. II. Title.
  KF320.A9L48   2013
  005.5'702434—dc23

                              2013006872

Discounts are available for books ordered in bulk. Special consideration is given to state bars, CLE programs, and other bar-related organizations. Inquire at Book Publishing, American Bar Association, 321 N. Clark Street, Chicago, Illinois 60654.

www.ShopABA.org

Contents

About the Authors .... *vii*

Acknowledgments .... *xi*

Foreword .... *xiii*

Introduction   xvii

The Google Apps Suite xvii

Security, Confidentiality, and Ethics xviii

Focus on the Practical Use by Lawyers xix

Why Use the Cloud-Based Google Apps Suite's Calendar and Gmail over
       Conventional Calendar and E-mail Software? xxi

Types of Google Accounts xxv

Conventions Used in This Book   xxix

LESSONS

Lesson 1 Getting Started with Gmail   **1**

Lesson 2 Inbox View   **9**

Lesson 3 Labels   **13**

Lesson 4 How to Manage and Display Messages   **23**

Lesson 5 Settings   **29**

Lesson 6 Searching the Full Text of Messages — 55

Lesson 7 Contacts and Tasks Manager — 57

Lesson 8 Offline Access to Your Gmail Messages — 65

Lesson 9 Google Chat/Google Talk and Google Hangout — 69

Lesson 10 Call Phone: Telephone Calls from Within Gmail — 79

Lesson 11 Migrating Existing E-mail Messages to Gmail — 81

Lesson 12 Getting Started with Google Calendar — 85

Lesson 13 Adding Events to Google Calendar — 89

Lesson 14 Editing Events You've Added to the Calendar — 95

Lesson 15 Searching for Events and Appointments in Your Google Calendar — 97

Lesson 16 Printing Your Calendar — 99

Lesson 17 Customizing Your Calendar with Settings — 103

Lesson 18 Accessing Google Calendar Without an Internet Connection — 111

Lesson 19 Dashboard — 115

Lesson 20 Google Vault | **131**

Lesson 21 Google Apps Marketplace and Chrome Web Store Plug-ins | **133**

Lesson 22 Security, Confidentiality, and Ethics | **137**

Appendix A What Is Cloud Computing? | **163**

Index | **167**

About the Authors

Mark Rosch is the Vice-President of Internet For Lawyers (IFL), an Internet research Continuing Legal Education (CLE) training company. He is co-author of six American Bar Association (ABA) Law Practice Management Section (LPM) books: *Google Gmail and Calendar in One Hour for Lawyers; Find Info Like a Pro, Volume 1: Mining the Internet's Publicly Available Resources for Investigative Research; Find Info Like a Pro, Volume 2: Mining the Internet's Public Records for Investigative Research; Google for Lawyers,* and two editions of *The Lawyer's Guide to Fact Finding on the Internet.* He has also written twelve editions of *The Cybersleuth's Guide to the Internet* (published by IFL Press). Mark is a nationally recognized speaker who has presented at: the Annual meetings of the ABA and the California State Bar; ABA TECHSHOW; and hundreds of state and local bar associations, companies, and law firms since 1999.

Mark is the developer and manager of the company's website and Editor of IFL's newsletter. Mark writes, speaks, and tweets about how to use the Internet for research and how the legal community can use technology more effectively. He is a member of the ABA and the Association of Continuing Legal Education (ACLEA). He serves on the ABA LPM Section's TECHSHOW Planning Board and previously was a member of the Section's State and Local Bar outreach Committee and served as Vice Chair of the Section's Education Committee. Mark has also served in various leadership positions within ACLEA. Prior to his career in CLE, he worked in various senior-level staff and consulting Marketing and Public Relations positions in the entertainment and consumer electronics industries. He earned his Bachelors Degree in Sociology from the Tulane University of Louisiana.

Carole Levitt is the founder and President of Internet For Lawyers (IFL), an Internet research Continuing Legal Education (CLE) training company. She is a skilled online searcher and nationally recognized speaker focusing on legal, public record, investigative, and business research. She has presented at numerous annual meetings of the American Bar Association (ABA) and the California State Bar; the ABA TECHSHOW; and hundreds of state and local bar associations, companies, and law firms since 1999. Prior to her career in CLE, Carole was a law librarian, legal research and writing professor, and California attorney.

She is co-author of six books published by the ABA Law Practice Management (LPM) Section: *Google Gmail and Calendar in One Hour for Lawyers; Find Info Like a Pro, Volume 1: Mining the Internet's Publicly Available Resources for Investigative Research; Find Info Like a Pro, Volume 2: Mining the Internet's Public Records for Investigative Research; Google for Lawyers,* and two editions of *The Lawyer's Guide to Fact Finding on the Internet.* She has also written twelve editions of *The Cybersleuth's Guide to the Internet* (published by IFL Press).

Carole is a member of the Association of Continuing Legal Education and the ABA. She has served on the ABA LPM Section's Publishing Board since 2003 and served four years on the Section's Executive Council. She served on the California State Bar LPM Section's Board for eight years, including a year as Vice Chair and one as Chair. She also served on the Executive Board of the Los Angeles County Bar LPM Section and was Vice President of the Southern California Association of Law Librarians. Carole was recently elected to the College of Law Practice Management.

Ms. Levitt was a regular contributor to the Los Angeles Lawyer magazine's "Computer Counselor" column for eight years and has also written for numerous magazines, newsletters, and websites, such as California

Lawyer, Trial, The Internet Lawyer, Computer and Internet Lawyer, Research Advisor, Nashville Lawyer, FindLaw, CEB Case N Point, and LLRX.

Ms. Levitt received her Juris Doctorate from The John Marshall Law School in Chicago, where she graduated with distinction and was a member of the school's law review. She earned her Bachelors in Political Science and her Masters in Library Science at the University of Illinois.

Acknowledgments

We would like to thank and commend the ABA LPM Publications staff (Denise Constantine, Lindsay Dawson, Kimia Shelby, and Laura Bolesta) for all their hard work in producing this book.

A huge thank-you goes to our peer-reviewer/tech guru, Burgess Allison and our project manager/security guru, Dave Ries, for all the hours of work they spent reading, critiquing, and advising us . . . to help us make this book even better.

Foreword

I've been using Google Apps for about 4.5 years—since 2009 when Google opened the Apps platform. Before then, my stuff was on a self-hosted Microsoft Exchange platform. I knew I wasn't backing up my stuff in the self-hosted Exchange environment, so I migrated to a cloud-based Exchange platform.

I liked hosted Exchange systems, which had anytime access, but I needed to be able to access my calendar, e-mail, and contacts anywhere at anytime, and I didn't want to fuss with syncing my handheld device each night before I left the office. These pay-to-play programs cost as much as $20 per month per user. I was paying $60 per month for my three users at the time I migrated over to Google Apps for Business.

My practice management program is a desktop-based program that stores my contacts and calendar and integrates with Microsoft Outlook, so I needed an easy and secure way to transfer information from my desktop to the cloud. Both the connection and the provider's service terms had to provide security. I also needed the system to sync with my devices whenever and wherever I had an Internet connection. Most of all, the system needed to be easy to migrate to. I decided to migrate to Google Apps to save money and unify my systems and services. At $50 per year per user, Google Apps was a bargain.

Migration to the Google Apps platform was quick and easy. The sync program, Google Apps Sync, integrates with Microsoft Outlook. Basically, connecting my desktop calendar, e-mail, and contacts was a matter of entering the username and remembering the password for my Google Apps account. Google Apps Sync set up an IMAP profile in Microsoft Outlook, and in a few minutes the calendar and contacts on my desktop were synced with my Google Apps account. In addition, the program runs seamlessly in the background so I can enter information on the go and it magically appears in my practice management program.

Android, Google's mobile device operating system, became an important tool in helping expand my mobile law practice. So, with each release of Android, Google Apps also becomes an even more integrated part of my practice. Android and Google Apps sync seamlessly together, allowing me to work away from the office on my Android tablet or smartphone. On most days, I use Gmail, Google Calendar, and Contacts to handle my tasks. I love how each of these applications has mobile and desktop features, so I can manage my information with or without my mobile device. With a quick connection to the Internet, I can see all of my information.

I love how Google Apps organizes my messages in Gmail, giving me easy access to long conversations. I can set up Gmail to import mail from other systems. Even better, I can send messages that look like they come from my other email address(es), rather than the Gmail identity. Clients and colleagues can't tell the difference, and I get to use my vanity email.

Hosted Exchange is great for sharing calendars among members of my firm, which was an important ability I looked for when I moved to Google Apps. Fortunately, Google Calendar gives me that ability. My staff and other colleagues can see and edit my calendar, thus giving me flexibility to be away from the office. Since my calendar syncs to the cloud, I can access the information from my mobile device or desktop computer. Google Calendar features color-coded scheduling, similar to Microsoft Office Outlook, which makes viewing and editing quick and easy.

There are some great apps that connect a Google Calendar to the outside world, and one of my favorites is YouCanBook.Me. This app allows clients to schedule appointments on your calendar. You can use the app under "normal" conditions for free, otherwise it will cost you $10 per month. You can find similar apps for Gmail, contacts, and marketing.

DocuSign is another app offered in the Google Apps Marketplace. DocuSign allows me to send documents to clients and colleagues for signature. I can't count the number of comments I get about how cool it is to receive a digital document for signature. Concern about the signature's validity is relatively minor since the enactment of the Uniform Electronic Transactions Act and the Electronic Signatures in Global and National Commerce Act.

Within the last three years, Google has attempted to become the go-to replacement for Microsoft Office, adding an office suite called Google Drive. Google Drive is free, and it allows users to upload, edit, and create documents, spreadsheets, presentations, or forms. Its capabilities are comparable to Microsoft Office programs, though they admittedly lack some of the flashier features. In a pinch, the Google Docs applications work fine, especially when your work is collaborative.

Some folks I discuss Google Apps with are concerned about security, especially because stuff is stored in "the cloud." In reality though, I'm actually less concerned about my Google Apps account than my non-Google accounts, like Facebook and Twitter. Google Apps offers strong encryption to protect data, and features two-step authentication to avoid unauthorized access.

Two-step authentication requires you to enter a code, usually from a text message, to log into your Google Apps account. You can set a "remember" preference for "safe" computers, and then enter the code manually into any other computers you use to access the account. Two-step authentication can also protect your Google Apps information when you're in a public environment.

I also love Gmail's fantastic spam filter, which catches about 98% of the spam messages sent to my account. What's more, I don't even worry about those messages since Gmail automatically deletes them after 30 days.

Not once have I regretted my migration to Google Apps. Since I'm not very diligent about protecting my information, I find it comforting that someone else is.

—Jeffrey Taylor, Principal in the Oklahoma City law firm
Absolute Legal Services, LLC.
http://www.absolutelawfirm.com

Introduction

The Google Apps Suite

The Google Apps suite is a collection of web-based software and tools that allow you to create, share, and store documents on the Internet and communicate online (http://www.google.com/enterprise/apps/business/products.html).

These include:

- **Gmail** (e-mail)
- Ancillary tools found within **Gmail**
  - **Hangout** (video conferencing for up to ten people)
  - **Call Phone** (using your computer to call someone's phone)
  - **Voice Calling** (using your computer to call someone's computer)
  - **Chat** (one-to-one text chat)

- **Google Calendar** (appointment calendar)
- **Google Docs** (word processing)
- **Google Spreadsheets** (spreadsheets)
- **Google Presentations** (slide presentations)
- **Forms** (such as client intake forms)
- **Sites** (websites)
- **Drive** (storage)

This book focuses on just two of the many tools in the Google Apps suite: Gmail (and its Ancillary tools listed above) and Calendar. Before you can make use of the Google Apps suite, you need to sign up for one of Google's seven types of accounts (which are explained beginning on page xxv).

Because these tools and the related document storage are all web-based and require little more than an Internet connection and a web browser to access, they are referred to as "cloud computing" applications (see Appendix A for a more detailed explanation of cloud computing).

PRACTICE TIP

Why We Use Google Apps for Our Law Office

Chad Burton, Principal in the seven-lawyer, Dayton, Ohio-based Burton Law firm, cites a number of reasons for switching his firm to Google Apps for Business. "We have a virtual law firm with lawyers working in a distributed manner around Ohio and North Carolina, and Google Apps makes it easy for everyone to connect," he said. "Google Apps integrates with our other practice management platforms—Clio and Box—and the $50 per year price point is excellent for what is provided."

Burton made the decision to switch his full service and virtual law firm to Google Apps for Business two to three years ago because of the "user interface, 25 GBs of storage, and up-time guarantee," he said. "I also like the ease of use with mobile devices, including iPhones and iPads, and also back when I unfortunately used a Blackberry."

Security, Confidentiality, and Ethics

Some of the first questions we get when discussing Google Apps are "What about the security, confidentiality, and ethics of the information stored in those documents and e-mails?" and "Is it secure enough for lawyers to use?" We wouldn't be writing this book for lawyers if the answer were no. (See Lesson 22 for a full discussion.) Even with the security measures Google has in place for Google Apps, you still have a responsibility to make your account as secure as is reasonably possible by using a strong, hard to guess, password and 2-step authentication to access your account. (See Lesson 19 for more details about 2-step authentication.) You should also continually focus on security in everyday use and consider additional security features as they become available.

Millions of corporations, small businesses, solo lawyers, large and small law firms, and federal, state, and local governments have "gone Google"—meaning that they have moved from hosting their own e-mail servers (and in some cases calendars and documents) to using Google Apps. Companies that have gone Google range from Konica Minolta and Jaguar to the solo law practice Craig Law Firm (North Carolina) and the twelve-office law firm Bradford & Barthel. Government users include the U.S. General Services Administration, the U.S. National Oceanic and Atmospheric Administration, the State of Wisconsin, the New Mexico Attorney General's Office, the City of Los Angeles, and the City of Pittsburgh.

"As a law firm handling confidential information for our clients, Bradford & Barthel takes security extremely seriously," said the firm's Director of Knowledge Strategy and Technology, Eric Hunter, in a guest post on the Official Google Enterprise Blog (http://linkon.in/VvM3pL). "We're responsible for private information on individuals and companies, and our best security option is Google Apps," he continued. "Google has many security features—SAS70 Type II certification and two-step verification included—that allow us to feel confident our data and the data of our clients is much safer than if we hosted it on premise."

Focus on the Practical Use by Lawyers

The book is designed as a step-by-step guide for lawyers to learn what features and functions are available in Gmail and Calendar, as well as some ancillary services including Google Chat, Hangout, and Call Phone. You will learn how other lawyers are already putting those tools to work in their practices, and be provided ideas on how you could put those tools to work in your practice.

In particular, the book focuses on these tools as accessed via the paid Google Apps for Business account (see page xxvi). However, the majority of features and functions we describe are also available to users with free Google Accounts. We primarily use our own Google Apps for Business account to illustrate how a law firm might integrate these tools into its practice.

While this book is not intended to be an implementation guide for IT professionals, we realize that some solo and small firm attorneys might actually be the IT person at their firm. Lesson 19 provides information for those attorneys. (Attorneys not managing their own Google accounts

---

PRACTICE TIP

Why We Use Google Apps for Our Law Office

"We used to run an on-site Microsoft Exchange Server for our e-mail and calendars. It worked okay," said Clayton Hasbrook, an associate at the Oklahoma City firm of Hasbrook and Hasbrook, a three-lawyer firm handling insurance law, employment law, and personal injury matters. (See his post on the firm's blog, "Injury Attorney Resource Center" at http://linkon.in/ VJuPoH). "Any time we had problems with it though, we'd have to call our tech guy.

"We ended up switching to Google Apps in 2009," he said. "The main reason I prefer Gmail to Outlook is that it groups everything by conversation. This saves time and is really easy to use. Plus, we've never had to call our tech guy about e-mail or calendar problems.

"For those in your office who swear by Outlook, they can still use it," he continued. "The back-end will be the only thing different. But it will generally be easier to log on from the Internet and sync your phones to it. We had people in our office that stayed with Outlook after we initially switched over. Within two weeks they were using Gmail full time."

can probably skip this lesson.) With that said, some of our step-by-step illustrations of the lesser-known features of Gmail could be useful to IT professionals as they deploy Google Apps in their firms and train their users.

Why Use the Cloud-Based Google Apps Suite's Calendar and Gmail over Conventional Calendar and E-mail Software?

For the law firm of Bradford & Barthel, "Technology like Google Apps and social applications are creating a culture where the legal industry is much more connected with clients and clients have much more access to information about the law," the firm's Hunter said in that same blog post (see page xix). "Our primary reason for investigating Google Apps back in 2009 was to start preparing our firm to keep up with this new culture of constant communication and to help employees enhance client relationships through better sharing and collaboration."

"Since we migrated to Google Apps in April 2010, we've made collaboration much easier and more efficient through the use of Google Sites, Google Docs, and shared Google calendars," Hunter added. "Our attorneys have found Google Apps to be intuitive and flexible."

From a practical, day-to-day perspective, the cloud-based Google Apps suite's Calendar and Gmail offer a number of advantages over conventional software as discussed below.

Access Your E-mail from Any Web-enabled Device, From Anywhere at Anytime

You can check and send e-mail or add events to your calendar using any device from anywhere, as long as it has an Internet connection. The device could be your laptop or desktop computer (or one at a hotel's business center). The device could also be almost any web-enabled mobile device such as Android, iOS (iPhone or iPad), BlackBerry, or Windows Phone using the device's dedicated Gmail application, or through a web browser.

> **USAGE TIP**
>
> **Using a Public Computer Like Those in a Hotel's Business Center Is Not Recommended**
>
> There have been a number of reported incidents of software and hardware clandestinely installed on business center computers that can steal passwords or confidential information on the computer before it travels over the encrypted connection. They range from hard-to-detect spyware installed on the computer's hard drive to a small keylogger device that can be plugged into the computer where it's concealed from view. Additionally, these public computers often are not securely configured and lack current security software.

Automatically Sync Your E-mails and Calendar

With conventional calendar and e-mail software, you may have to install software on each device and then manually sync your data frequently. With Google Calendar and Gmail, you do not need to install any software and you do not need to manually sync any of your devices; it happens automatically because the suite tools and your data live in the cloud.

> **USAGE TIP**
>
> Even without an Internet connection, you may be able to at least view your Gmail messages and your Calendar (see Lessons 2 and 18, respectively, for details).

Integrate with Practice Management Software

As practice management software has evolved, vendors of traditional and cloud-based practice management software have built-in the ability to integrate messages and/or appointments from Gmail and Google Calendar into their products. Some of the most popular of these include **Abacus** (http://www.abacuslaw.com), **Advologix** (http://www.advologix.com), **Clio** (http://www.goclio.com), **HoudiniESQ** (http://www.houdiniesq.com), **MyCase** (http://www.mycase.com), and **Rocket Matter** (http://www.rocketmatter.com).

When discussing Rocket Matter's integration with Google Calendar, company CEO and Founder Larry Port explained, "Our Google Calendar integration is a full-two way sync and allows users to leverage Google's powerful calendaring tools and Rocket Matter's billing capabilities. The two-way sync supports advanced functionality like recurring events, alarms and notifications, and coordination across all attendees of an event," for example. "Since Google Calendar integrates with a variety of software and devices, Rocket Matter two-way synching extends to those platforms as well: an event created in Rocket Matter will show up in Outlook, Apple's iCal, or Android, iPhone, and iPad mobile devices," he continued.

Save Money

- The Google Apps accounts range from free to $50 or $100 per user per year (as of this writing), depending on which type of account you select (see page xxv, Types of Google Accounts) vs. the $200 price for one copy of Microsoft Office Home and Business.
- There are no upgrade costs. When new features and functions are introduced to the Google Apps suite, they appear automatically.
- You may be able to reduce your IT expenses because Google's engineers are maintaining the servers that handle your mail.

The Health and Security of the Servers That House Your Data Are Monitored 24/7

Google's engineering staff:

- Regularly update their servers to include the most up-to-date security patches.
- Continually test their servers' hard-drives and replace them before they fail, so you don't lose any of your data.
- Create redundant back-ups of your data to guard against loss.
- Physically secure their data centers with fences, guards, and key card and biometric access.
- Give random file names to "data chunks" and do not store the data in clear text, which makes them not humanly readable to anyone but you and those with whom you share the document.

Gmail Provides You with Large Storage Space for Your Messages and Offers Large File-Attachment Limits

Free Gmail accounts and free Google Apps Accounts now come with 10 gigabytes (GB) of storage space for e-mail messages and attachments. You can upgrade a free account to 25 GB for $2.49/month, but Google Apps for Business accounts already come with 25 GB of storage space as part of the $5 per user monthly fee.

Gmail Provides Strong Spam-Filtering

Regardless of how you access your messages (e.g., from your laptop, your phone, Outlook . . .), you will benefit from Gmail's strong spam-filtering capabilities.

Google Provides Powerful Search and Retrieval Capability for Gmail and Calendar

Because Gmail and Calendar are operated by Google—a well-known and powerful search engine for the web, they benefit from the same powerful search-and-retrieval capability when you are trying to find a message, an attachment, or an event. Many of these advantages are discussed in detail later in Lesson 6.

Types of Google Accounts

There are seven account types you can create to access the tools described in this book (see Figure I.1).

The type that you're probably most familiar with is the free consumer **Gmail Account** (e.g., mrosch@gmail.com). This type of account is meant for the personal use of one individual. If you have a Gmail address, you already have access to the free versions of these tools. To set up a Gmail account if you don't already have one, visit http://www.gmail.com. All e-mail and documents created in this consumer version are connected to a generic username@gmail.com address (e.g., mrosch@gmail.com).

Beyond the free consumer **Gmail Account**, there are six other types of accounts for accessing Gmail, some free and some paid. They are intended for business use and are called:

- **Google Apps.** (Free.) You can customize these tools for your own Internet domain name (e.g., netforlawyers.com), with up to 10 users with a customized e-mail address (mrosch@netforlawyers. com). Note that as of December 2012, new customers can no longer create these types of free accounts, but they will remain free to those who had already created them.

- **Google Apps for Business.** (Paid; $5 per user (for an unlimited number of users) per month or $50 per user per year when automatically billed to a credit card.) While similar to the free Google Apps version, this type of account adds greater storage capacity, additional security features for mobile devices, dedicated technical support, and certain service guarantees.
- **Google Apps for Business with Vault.** (Paid.) An additional $5 per user per month adds the **Vault** corporate message retention, governance, and compliance tool (discussed in Lesson 20) to a Google Apps for Business account.
- **Google Apps for Education.** (Free.) This account is the same as the Google Apps for Business account, but it is provided for free to selected educational institutions.
- **Google Apps for Government.** (Paid.) Available to governmental agencies, this account is the same as the Google Apps for Business account.
- **Google Apps for Non-Profits.** (Free.) Provided for free to selected non-profit organizations, this account is the same as the Google Apps for Business account.

All of these accounts work the same way and offer the same level of security. However, the paid accounts offer a few additional features, such as more technical support, more storage space, guarantees of service (a.k.a. uptime), and the ability to disable ads in Gmail, among others. Therefore, while we've stated that this book focuses on these tools as accessed via the paid Google Apps for Business account, the information is applicable no matter which type of account you are using. One small difference between the free and paid accounts is that the free account uses the label "Gmail" for e-mail messages while the paid account uses the label "Mail." Depending on which account was used when we took screen shots, you will see one or the other.

Figure I.1 Google Account Comparison

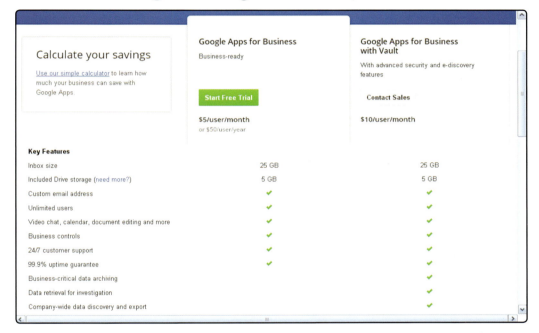

(http://www.google.com/enterprise/apps/business/pricing.html)

Which Type of Account Is Appropriate for Lawyers?

We used to recommend that solos and small firms begin by using the free Google Apps Account to test drive the service and that larger firms and government agencies begin with Google Apps for Business from the outset. But, as noted earlier, the free Google Apps Account no longer exists for new users, so all lawyers will need to sign up for the Google Apps for Business account. Even with its (minimum) $50 per user per year price tag, it can still be a big cost-saver compared with other e-mail service providers. It's also a good choice because it comes with technical support while the free account did not. Fortunately, Google Apps for Business offers a thirty-day free trial for you to evaluate the service. For those who created a free Google Apps Account before Google ceased offering it, conversion from the free Google Apps Account to the paid Google Apps for Business account is seamless.

Conventions Used in This Book

Throughout the book we use **boldfaced** type to indicate exact text that appears onscreen in links, buttons, drop-down menus, labels, etc., for the features and tools we discuss (e.g, **Compose**, **Attach a file**) as well as the first instance of key terms. Additionally, we use italics to indicate exact text (search terms/keywords) typed for sample searches.

Throughout this book we offer **Practice Tips** from lawyers who are using Google Apps in their practice and **Usage Tips** that are more general.

PRACTICE TIP

Before using any cloud computing service provider, lawyers should make a reasonable effort to insure that confidential client information stored on those systems will remain confidential. The recent addition of a new Paragraph (c) to ABA Model Rule 1.6 (**http://linkon.in/OYJllc**) reads, "A lawyer shall make reasonable efforts to prevent the inadvertent disclosure of, or unauthorized access to, information relating to the representation of a client." Lesson 22 of this book looks at security practices Google has put in place for the information stored in Google Apps and surveys State Bar ethics opinions related to cloud computing services.

USAGE TIP

If you sign into Gmail from multiple computers, but are worried you may have forgotten to sign out of one, you can sign out remotely. At the bottom of your Inbox, you'll see information about the time and location of the last activity on your account. Click **Details** to see whether your account is still open in another location and **Sign out all other sessions** to close all other open sessions. Also see the Usage Tip, *Using a Public Computer like Those in a Hotel's Business Center is Not Recommended*, on page xxii, warning against using public computers.

Lesson 1

Getting Started with Gmail

We hope you didn't skip the Introduction. Before you learn about the mechanics of how to get started with Gmail, you will want to first learn about the benefits you will derive from using it . . . and that's all in the Introduction.

Accessing Gmail

We assume that if you are reading this book that you probably have already set up some type of Google Account as described in the Introduction. If you have not signed up for an account, see Section 19, Signing up for Your Google Apps Account, on page 116.

Gmail can be accessed either via its robust web-based Inbox interface or through your favorite e-mail client, such as Microsoft Outlook or Mozilla Thunderbird. If you prefer to receive your Gmail messages in Outlook or some other e-mail client, Google has created a step-by-step guide to set up your e-mail client at http://mail.google.com/support/bin/topic.py?topic=12912.

If you have multiple e-mail users in your office, each of them can choose whether to use Gmail's web-based Inbox interface or their favorite e-mail client. For example, Mark prefers to receive his messages in Gmail's web-based Inbox because it has powerful search-and-retrieval capabilities and he can access his e-mails (and any attachments) from anywhere he can get an Internet connection. Carole prefers to receive her messages in Outlook, where she takes advantage of some of Outlook's organizational features to keep track of her messages, projects, appointments, and so on, but she also uses Gmail's web-based Inbox for the same reasons Mark does.

If you're already using an e-mail client such as Outlook and opt to receive your Gmail messages there, you will find no differences in how you send, receive, and search those messages in Outlook. For this reason, we'll focus only on Gmail's web-based Inbox, which is specific to Gmail. If you decide

> **PRACTICE TIP**
>
> Dayton, Ohio-based business and litigation lawyer Chad Burton prefers to use Gmail via his Web browser, "because the interface is so smooth," he said. "I use Labels, Chat, Filters, and several of the Lab features on a regular basis."

that you want to switch from your existing e-mail client to managing your messages in Gmail's web-based Inbox, Google offers tools and instructions to migrate your existing messages and folder structure (see Lesson 11).

How to Compose Messages

In November 2012, Google changed the way in which messages are composed. While Google offers you a choice to **Switch back to old compose**, by the time you read this book, that choice may not exist, so we only discuss the new way to compose.

1. Click the red **Compose** link at the top of the left-hand column of the **Inbox**.

2. A small blank **New Message** pops up in the bottom right-hand corner of the **Inbox**—Google no longer navigates you away from your **Inbox** (see Figure 1.1).

Lesson 1 Getting Started with Gmail **3**

Figure 1.1 Small Compose Window

3. If you don't like using this small **New Message** pop-up, click on the arrow located on the top right-hand corner (where the words *pop-out* appear) of the pop-up, and a new compose window appears that you can make larger (see Figure 1.2). However, if you are

Figure 1.2 Large Compose Window

using a different browser than the one displayed in Figures 1.1 and 1.2 (version 24 of Chrome), a new tab may pop up instead of a new window.

4. After you type your message, you can **Save & Close** (this saves the message to your **Drafts**, but this option only appears when you are viewing the small **New Message** pop-up).

   If you hover over the **X** in the larger **New Message** compose window, the word **Close** will pop up (instead of the words **Save and Close** that pop up in the small blank New Message compose window). Nevertheless, if you click the **X** (before sending your message), it will still be saved to your **Drafts** and not deleted.

5. You can send your message by clicking the blue **Send** link.

6. As in most word processing software, Gmail gives you **Formatting options**, e.g., **B** (boldface), **I** (italicize), etc., by clicking the *A* button.

7. You can also **Attach Files** by clicking the paperclip icon (see pages 5–7 for information about attachments).

8. By choosing the + icon, you can **Insert Photos** or **Insert Link** into the message. Google often adds or changes features. For instance, while writing this book we noticed an **Insert invitation (coming soon)** icon when we clicked on the + icon. A few weeks later, *coming soon* had been deleted from the Insert invitation icon, indicating this feature now works. So, you can now insert an invitation into your message

> **USAGE TIP**
>
> **How's Your Spelling?**
> Gmail will automatically check your spelling and underline (in red) words that are misspelled.

Lesson 1 Getting Started with Gmail   **5**

(e.g., to a client reminding them of a meeting, deposition, etc.). The invitation automatically will be placed in your Google calendar as an event.

9. Clicking the trash icon allows you to **Discard Draft**.

10. Hidden behind the down-arrow are **More Options**, such as **Switch back to old compose** or **Print**.

USAGE TIP

Making the Gmail Web Interface Your Default Method for Sending E-mails

Until now, clicking on an e-mail link on the Web or in any application would open the composition window in the default e-mail program on your computer (e.g., Outlook in Windows, Mail in Mac OS). That default annoyed those who preferred to manage their Gmail Inbox in their Web browser because there was no option to set the default to open the Gmail browser-based composition window.

After downloading, installing, and setting the Google Notifier software (http://linkon.in/NMQWWE), clicking on e-mail links in any application (not just on the web) on your computer opens a new Gmail message composition window in your web browser.

Note that if you're using the Google Chrome Web browser, the process is different. It is described at http://linkon.in/TcwWDy.

How to Attach a File to a Gmail Message

You can easily attach any file on your computer (up to 25 megabytes) to a Gmail message by following the three steps in Figure 1.3. The file is then automatically attached to the message. Repeat the same three steps if you need to add more files from other folders.

6 Google Gmail and Calendar in One Hour for Lawyers

You can also attach multiple files from the same folder to a message. On a Windows operating system computer, hold down the **Control** key and left-click each file you want to attach (or to attach a continuous group of files, hold down the **Shift** key). On a Mac OS computer, hold down the **Command** key and click each file you want to attach. If you're using the Chrome browser (in either operating system), you can drag files from your computer right into the body of e-mail to attach them. If you need to delete an attachment after it's been attached, simply click the X to the right of the file name.

Figure 1.3 Attaching a File

Gmail automatically recognizes phrases such as *I've attached*, *I'm attaching*, *attached is*, etc., in the body of your message to help keep you from forgetting to attach files you intended to. If Gmail detects one of these phrases in a message, but there is no file attached to the message when you click the **Send** button, you are prompted with a pop-up box (see Figure 1.4). You can select **Cancel** to cancel sending the message that is missing the attachment and then attach the missing file, or you can select **OK** to send the message without an attachment.

Figure 1.4 Prompt to Attach a File

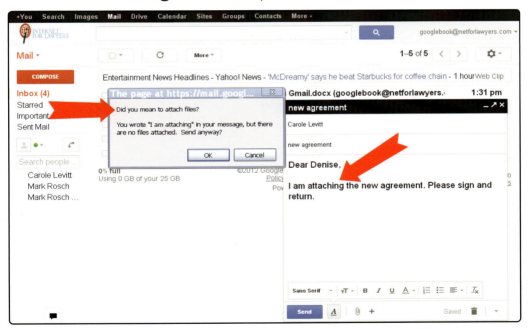

Lesson 2

Inbox View

Conversation View

One major difference between Gmail and most e-mail software is the way Gmail groups messages with the same subject line into "conversations" by default (also referred to as "threads" by other e-mail programs). As a new message is added to the conversation, the sender's name, subject line, etc., are boldfaced (indicating that the message is unread) and the message moves to the top of the reverse-chronological list of messages (see Figure 2.1). The conversation view can be turned off if you prefer viewing individual messages in reverse chronological order. The Gmail Inbox will then look similar to other stand-alone and web-based e-mail software.

Regardless of the view you decide to use, the Inbox's other attributes remain the same: the identity of the message's sender, a snippet of text from the beginning of the message, the time of receipt (if received today) or date (if not received today), and icons showing what type of document is attached (e.g., the paperclip icon shown in Figure 2.1, or other icons, such as a calendar, to show that the message includes an invitation that has been added to your calendar).

The first conversation in Figure 2.1 contains seven messages from various dates. Clicking the subject line displays each of the messages in

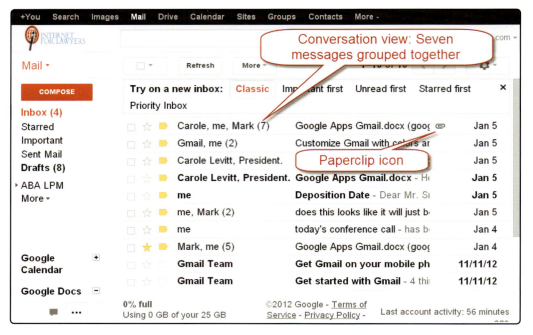

Figure 2.1 Conversation View of Inbox (Classic)

that one conversation in reverse-chronological order. The paperclip icon indicates that there is a document attachment (e.g., a Word document or a spreadsheet).

Figure 2.2 shows how we changed the default Conversation Inbox's Classic view to show the **Important** (messages) **first**, with all other messages placed in a separate section labeled **Everything else**. You can also change the view to display **Unread first**, **Starred first**, or **Priority Inbox** by clicking any of them in the **Try on a new inbox** section. If you do not see the **Try on a new inbox** message, you should hover over the **Inbox** label in the left-hand column (beneath **Compose**) and a drop-down arrow will appear. Click the arrow to choose one of the new Inbox views.

You can opt out of reviewing new messages in a specific conversation by muting the conversation. To do so, click the checkbox to the left of the

Figure 2.2 Conversation View of Inbox (Important First)

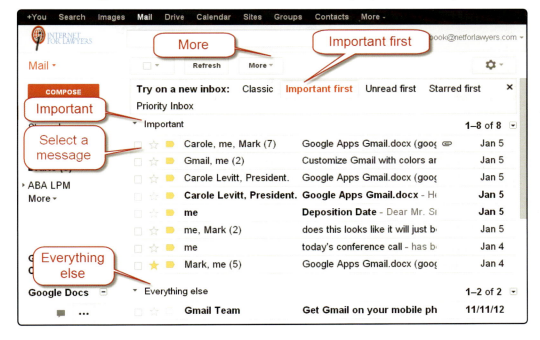

conversation and then more options will appear, including a new **More** tab with a longer drop-down menu (see Figure 2.3). Select **Mute** from the **More** drop-down menu. Note that messages in muted conversations are not deleted, they are just moved from your Inbox to your **All Mail** folder—any subsequent messages in that conversation will also be automatically routed to the All Mail folder without appearing in your Inbox. Of course, people often reply to a previous message with a new message on a completely different topic without changing the old subject line. So be aware that any automated filtering like this can hide what turns out to be an important new message. Fortunately, muted conversations can always be retrieved in searches of All Mail. You can also apply **Filter messages like these** to a label (folder) of your choice instead of selecting **Mute** to opt out of reviewing new messages in a specific conversation.

12 Google Gmail and Calendar in One Hour for Lawyers

Figure 2.3 Mute Conversation

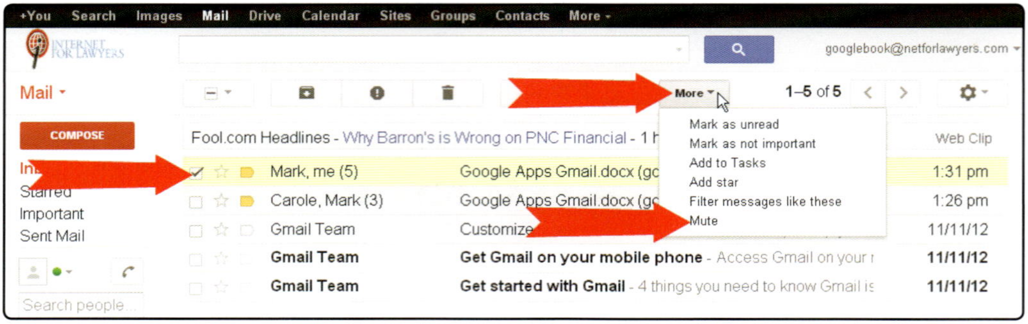

Conversation View Turned Off

When the conversation view is turned off, e-mail messages are displayed in reverse chronological order, with the most recently received message displayed at the top of the list. Messages that appear in bold typeface are unread, and those not in bold typeface have already been read (see Figure 2.4).

Figure 2.4 Conversation View Off

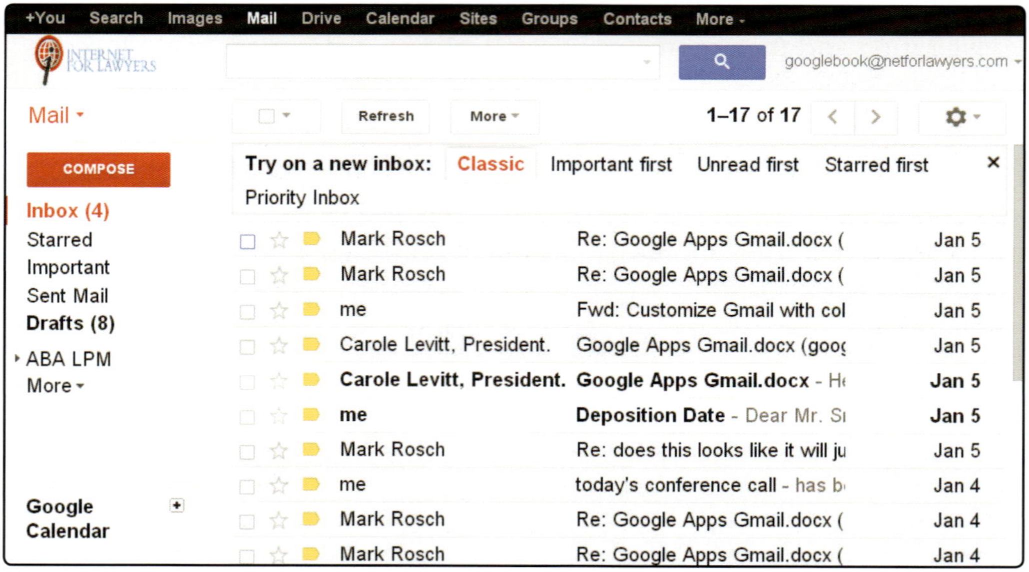

Lesson 3

Labels

While other e-mail service software providers allow you to move a message into a "folder," Gmail allows you to categorize or "label" a message. Like newer versions of Outlook, Gmail allows you to assign as many labels as you want to any given message. Labels are displayed in the left-hand column beneath the red Compose button.

> **USAGE TIP**
>
> Labeling is an important feature for e-mail—many lawyers find that labeling helps them better organize their e-mail. It lets the lawyer zero in on e-mails that are especially important or that contain critical action items or due dates, or even separate personal e-mail from work e-mail. Of course, the traditional method of organizing e-mails has been to store them in named folders. But that forces you to store an e-mail in a single folder, when many attributes may apply. Labeling lets you identify a single e-mail as coming from the Court, related to a particular matter, containing an action item, and assigned to a certain colleague. Later, when the action item is complete, you can simply remove that label without having to move the message around.

Gmail has two different types of labels, listed in the left-hand column beneath the **Compose** button (see Figure 3.1). System Labels are the default labels that Google has pre-set for you (the existing list begins with **Inbox** and ending with **Trash** as seen in Figure 3.1). Custom Labels are those you create.

Figure 3.1 Pre-Set System Labels

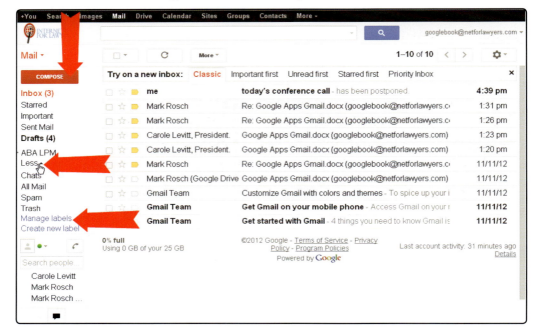

Regardless of which Inbox view you select or whether you turn the Conversation View on or off, the system labels and the custom labels are the same. Lesson 3 discusses ways to manage and create labels.

To display the full spectrum of labels and other tools, you need to click the **More** link in the left-hand column (see Figure 2.4 beneath the "ABA LPM" label). Once you click the More link, it changes it to a **Less** link (as shown in Figure 3.1) and beneath that more labels (e.g., **All mail**, **Spam** and tools (e.g., **Manage labels**) are displayed.

System Labels

All system labels, except for the Inbox system label, can be hidden. However, System labels cannot be removed or altered. Custom labels can be removed. In this lesson, each System label displayed in the left-hand column of Figure 3.1 will be discussed, and we'll explain how to create custom labels, manage labels, and delete a label from a message.

Inbox Label

Clicking any of the labels in the Inbox's left-hand column allows you to view messages assigned to that label. The Inbox label is the first stop for a message after it's received unless you have created **Filters**, in which case the Inbox is bypassed (see Lesson 5, page 44).

Starred Label

The second link, the **Starred** label, displays all messages you have starred. "Starring" is something that you do yourself by clicking into the clear star to the left of the message ☆, which turns the star yellow ⭐. (See Lesson 5, pages 35–36 for information about changing the colors of stars.) Obviously, you can decide to use the starring for any purpose that suits your needs—maybe it's for action items, or e-mails from a Court or regulatory agency. It's up to you.

Important Label

The third link, the **Important** label, is one that Google assigns automatically, usually based on keywords it detects in the message, people involved in the conversation, or interaction with a long thread. The Important messages are indicated by a yellow arrow to the right of the star ▱. Some of those arrows might have one or two chevrons within the arrow. The more chevrons, the more important Google thinks the message is. If you hover over the yellow arrow, a pop-up explains why Google thinks it's important. You can also help Google "learn" what's important by clicking the yellow arrow to turn it clear (to tell Google it's not an important e-mail) or by clicking the clear arrow to turn it to yellow (to tell Google that it is an important e-mail).

While this is a valuable feature, recognize that Google's algorithm for determining importance may not match your view of importance (e.g., some e-mails may be assigned a high importance because the Sender marked it as important). That's why some lawyers use the Star labels, or another custom label, for what they decide is really important. Again, this is up to you.

Sent Mail Label

The fourth link, the **Sent** Mail label, contains all of the messages sent from your account.

Drafts Label

The fifth link, the **Drafts** label, contains messages in progress. Clicking the **Save Now** button while you're composing a message saves it to the Drafts label for later retrieval.

Circles Label

The sixth link, the **Circles** label, is fairly new and is one of the ways Google is integrating features from its Google+ social network into Gmail. Circles are groupings of people you create from your contacts in Google+. If you click on the word **Circles**, it shows a list of the circles you created in Google+ (e.g., **Friends**, **Family**, **Law School**, etc.). Clicking one of the circles displays all the messages from people in that particular circle. If you click the drop-down arrow to the right of the Circles label, a pop-up menu offers you the opportunity to **Hide**, **Edit**, or **Show** the Circles label.

Chats

Chats, although listed in the middle of the labels, isn't really a label. It's a "gadget" discussed in Lesson 9.

All Mail Label

The seventh link, the **All Mail** label, contains all of the messages you've received, even those you've moved out of your Inbox (into other labels) or those in your Trash.

Spam Label

The eighth link, the **Spam** label, contains messages that Google automatically detects as spam and assigns the Spam label. Gmail does a very good job of blocking spam, but sometimes it goes into overdrive and assigns the Spam label to non-spam messages. We recommend frequently perusing the messages that have been automatically assigned the Spam label to search for messages that are not spam, because Google deletes the Spam messages that are more than 30 days old. If you find non-spam messages that have been assigned the Spam label, you should definitely click the checkbox to the left of the message and then click the **Not spam** button near the top of the window. This instructs Gmail *not* to treat future messages from this sender as spam and automatically moves the selected message to the Inbox.

Trash Label

The ninth link, the **Trash** label, is where you can send messages you no longer want to keep. You can click on the **Empty Trash now** link once you select the **Trash** label or you can just rely on Google to take out the Trash—Google automatically deletes messages labeled Trash that are more than 30 days old.

> **PRACTICE TIP**
>
> If you have moved a message to the **Trash** by accident or later decide that you do need to keep it, you can open the message in the Trash label and then click the **Move to** drop-down menu and select the label into which you want to move it.

How to Create Custom Labels

You can create your own labels by clicking the **Create new label** link in the left-hand column (you'll probably have to click **More** to see it) and typing the name for your new label into the pop-up box that appears (see Figure 3.2). Clicking the **Create** button adds your new label to the label list. You can create sub-labels (like sub-folders) by selecting **Nest label under** and selecting a **Parent** (label). Figure 3.2 shows the label we created for *Google Apps in One Hour*. We then selected **Nest label under** the parent *ABA LPM* so that *Google Apps in One Hour* became a sub-label of *ABA LPM*. We later created a new sub-sub-label, *Gmail*, to be nested under the sub-label *Google Apps in One Hour*.

Figure 3.2 Custom Nested Labels

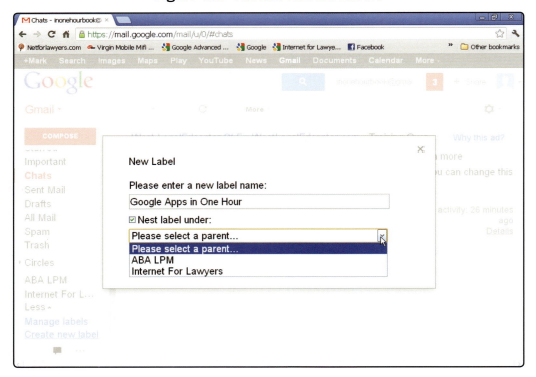

Lesson 3 Labels

How to Manage Labels (System and Custom)

You can manage both system and custom labels by clicking the **Manage labels** link in the left-hand column of the Gmail web interface (see Figure 3.1). You will then be taken to the Labels tab in Settings (see Figure 3.3). The Inbox system label is the only label you cannot manage; it is always displayed. Other system labels can be hidden, but realize that hiding a label only moves it to the **More** area (see Figure 2.4). For the **Drafts** label, you have an extra choice: **show if unread**. Once you click **More**, the so-called hidden labels appear (you can never delete the system labels). You definitely have more control over managing custom labels; you can show, hide, edit, or remove them completely.

Figure 3.3 Manage Labels

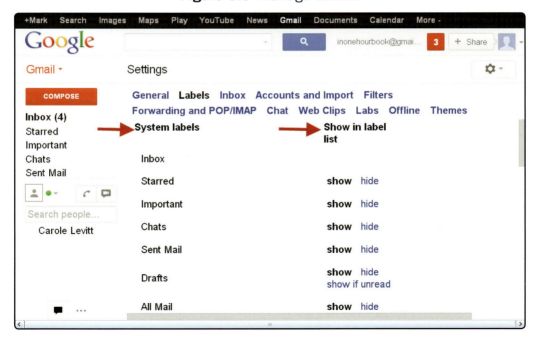

Deleting a Label from a Message

When you view your Inbox or open a message, all assigned labels are displayed unless you have chosen to hide them (see Figure 3.4b). You can click the **X** next to a label to remove it (see Figure 3.4a). If you removed all labels, the message would still be available in All Mail. Figure 3.4a shows that we have assigned different colors to our labels. You do this by hovering over the label in the left-hand column and clicking the drop-down arrow when it appears to the right of the label name.

Figure 3.4a Delete Label

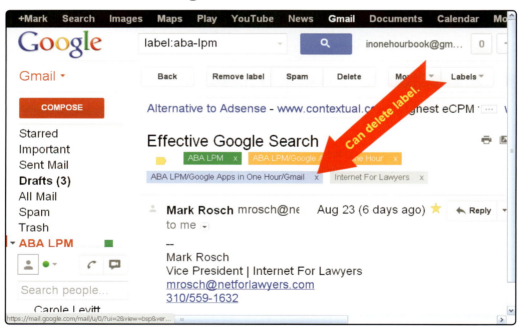

Lesson 3 Labels **21**

Adding Label Colors and Managing Labels

A pop-up box offers you a choice of colors for your label (see Figure 3.4b). From this pop-up you can also choose to show or hide labels (in the label list or the Inbox message list), edit or remove labels, and add sub-labels.

Figure 3.4b Adding Label Colors

Lesson 4

How to Manage and Display Messages

Managing your messages is one of the most powerful features that an e-mail system can offer you. In a business world that runs on e-mail, being able to quickly focus on all the e-mails related to a particular topic or quickly find an e-mail that contains a critical attachment or deadline can affect your efficiency dramatically.

Manage Groups of Messages

You can manage groups of messages or just one message in a variety of ways.

While you are viewing the Gmail Inbox list of messages, notice the unmarked box (see Figure 4.1a) located at the top left of the Inbox (above the messages). If you hover over the down arrow next to the unmarked box, the word **Select** appears. If you then click on the down arrow, a drop-down menu (see Figure 4.1b) allows you to choose **All, Read, Unread, Starred,** or **Unread**. Once you've made a selection, a check mark is inserted into the box next to each message that meets the criteria you selected. You can uncheck all of the messages that you selected by clicking the link **None** from the unmarked **Select** drop-down menu.

24   Google Gmail and Calendar in One Hour for Lawyers

Figures 4.1a–b Selecting Groups of Messages

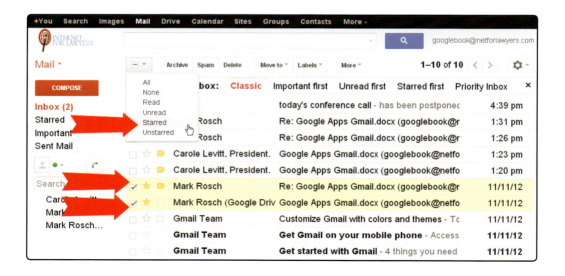

Once checkmarks have been inserted into the box next to each message that meets the criteria you selected, various buttons (**Archive**, **Spam**, **Delete**, **Move to**, **Labels**, and **More**) are displayed, allowing you to manage all of the selected messages as a group instead of one by one (see Figure 4.1b).

For example, we might assign the group of starred messages a new "Follow up on Monday" customized label by clicking on **Labels** and selecting that label, or we might move our group of read messages into the **Archive**. The Archive button cleans up your Inbox by moving selected messages from your Inbox to your All Mail label (which con-

> **PRACTICE TIP**
>
> In theory, your Inbox should be reserved for items that you're currently working on. Messages that contain completed action items should be assigned to a corresponding Label. If no logical Label exists, but you still want to keep the message, you can place it in the Archive. That way it won't clutter up your Inbox.

tains all of the messages you've received, even those in your Trash).

Manage an Individual Message

After you open and read a message from someone, you have many options for handling the message (see Figure 4.2). You can reply by selecting the **Reply** button, or you can click the drop-down arrow to the right of **Reply** to reveal the menu that allows you to forward, delete, and so on. A **Reply all** choice only appears on this menu when the email involves more than one recipient.

The row of buttons to the right of the red **Mail** allows you to go **Back** (to the message list), **Archive** (the message), report the message as **Spam** which also automatically assigns the Spam label to future messages from the same sender (this can also be undone if you decide it's not spam; see page 17 in Lesson 3 for more information), **Delete (**the message), **Move** (the message) **to**, add **Labels** (see Lesson 3) and take **More** actions.

If you select **More**, a drop-down menu would display where you could choose one of the following actions: **Mark as Unread, Mark as not important, Filter messages like these, Add to Tasks, Add Star, Create event** (see the Usage Tip on page 27), or **Mute**.

Figure 4.2 Handling an Opened Message

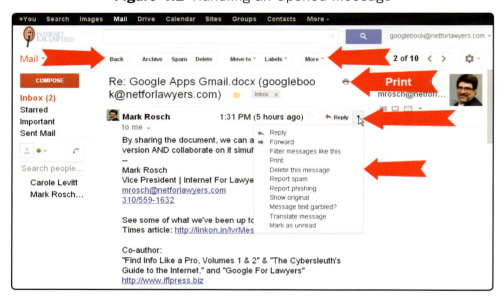

> **USAGE TIP**
>
> **Printing a Message**
>
> The typewriter icon shown in Figure 4.2 allows you to print the content of the message without any of the ads or the right and left-hand columns.

As you view an opened e-mail, you can hover over the down-arrow beneath the sender's name and the words **Show details** appear (see Figure 4.3). Selecting this option reveals additional information from the e-mail's header, such as the sender's e-mail address, which can be helpful in determining if a message is really from the person whose name appears in the e-mail.

Lesson 4 How to Manage and Display Messages **27**

> ### USAGE TIP
>
> ## Adding Events to Your Calendar Directly from Gmail
> Using the **Create event** option mentioned above (in the list of **More** actions that can be taken when handling a message), you can turn any e-mail message that you've received into an event on any of your Google calendars. This opens a new event that automatically inserts the e-mail subject as the event title. The text of the e-mail automatically becomes the description and you and any e-mail recipients are automatically added as guests. One down side to this method is it only allows you to add the event to the default calendar for that particular e-mail address. However, after you save the event, you can then edit any of its parameters, including moving it to any of your other calendars.

Figure 4.3 Show Sender's Details

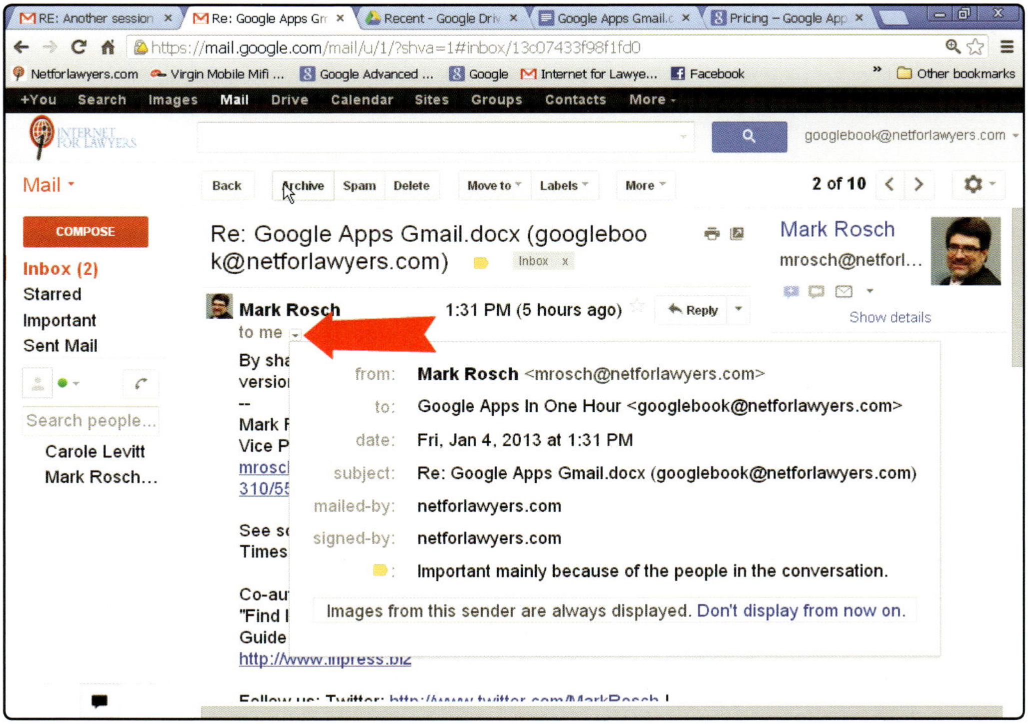

As you scroll down a message, you can choose to download specific attachments or all of them. You can quickly preview the attachment (instead of downloading and opening it) by clicking the **View** link at the bottom of the message to open a preview of the attachment in a new window. However, you will first need to enable **Previews** (see Lesson 5, page 42).

If you have chosen to show the **People Widget** (see Lesson 5 for an explanation), the right-hand column shows all kinds of information about the person who sent you the e-mail (see Figure 4.4).

Figure 4.4 Downloading and Previewing Attachments

See Lesson 5, page 31 for details about other items labeled in Figure 4.4.

Lesson 5

Settings

You can customize the look and feel of your Gmail account (and add cool gadgets) with the controls that you'll find by clicking the unlabeled "**Gear**" **Icon** ⚙ located in the upper right-hand side of your Inbox (see Figure 5.1), selecting **Settings** and then selecting one of the eight

Figure 5.1 Google Settings

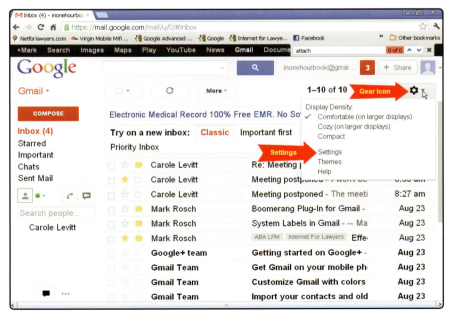

tabs (see Figure 5.2): **General**, **Accounts and Import**, **Labels**, **Filters**, **Forwarding and POP/IMAP, Chat**, **Web Clips**, and **Labs**. Underneath Settings (see Figure 5.1) is a **Themes** option (which allows you to change the background of your Gmail) and a **Help** option to locate articles on specific topics related to using Gmail.

Gmail General Settings

When you select Settings, the first page to appear is the **General Settings tab** (see Figure 5.2), which controls much of the look and feel of your Gmail Web interface, as well as some of its special features. While

Figure 5.2 Gmail Settings

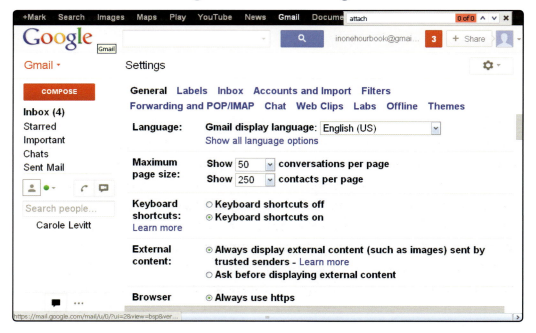

settings like **Language**, **Maximum page size, Signature,** and **Vacation responder** are pretty self-explanatory, some of the others may not be so clear, such as **Keyboard shortcuts**, **External content**, and **Browser**, all of which we'll explain in Lesson 5. We'll also explain several other **General Setting**s options in Lesson 5.

Be sure to scroll down to the bottom of the page to learn if you need to save your changes. You'll see a **Save Changes** button if you do need to affirmatively save your changes (some of the Tabs do not require this step).

Keyboard Shortcuts

Keyboard shortcuts allow you to invoke many of the service's features and functions with predetermined keystrokes, rather than clicking buttons and icons in the web interface. For example, simply selecting the "**c**" key opens a new message, while **Shift + c** opens a new message in a new window. You can see the full list of these shortcuts at http://linkon.in/OJh2KY.

External Content

When you receive a message with external content such as images, Gmail does not display it in the message, but instead includes two links at the top. Clicking the first link, **Display images below**, approves the display of the content in just that one message. Clicking the second link, **Always display images from sender@sender.com** designates that sender to be a "trusted sender." The **External content** option in the **General Settings** lets you pre-determine whether you want to display externally linked content, such as images, in the messages you receive from specific "trusted senders." To always display images in messages from these trusted senders, click the option **Always display external content (such as images) sent by trusted senders**.

> ### USAGE TIP
>
> **Why Block External Content?**
>
> Blocking external content from automatically loading in your e-mails can protect your e-mail account and your computer.
>
> Today, the primary purpose of blocking external content, such as images, is to protect your e-mail from spammers. Spammers embed images in the messages they send as a tracking mechanism. When they detect that an image has been downloaded, that tells them that the message they sent to you was opened and read—confirming that yours is a valid e-mail address. Additionally, malicious software (aka malware) can be embedded in images or other external elements that might get "opened" along with the spammer's message, doing damage to your computer.

Browser

If you've never changed this setting, no radio buttons are selected. However, because the default is **Always Use HTTPS** (Hypertext Transfer Protocol Secure), you have already been using that option without knowing it. You can change this option to **Don't Always Use HTTPS**, but we don't recommend it because Always Use HTTPS provides you with secure (encrypted) communication even when you are using Gmail via a non-secure Internet connection, such as a public wireless connection or a non-encrypted network.

Desktop Notifications and Button Labels (Changing Icons to Text)

You can turn notifications of new e-mail and chat messages on (you are notified with a pop-up on your desktop) or off.

The buttons at the top of messages displayed in the browser can be switched from **Icons** to **Text** through an option under **General Settings**.

My Picture and People Widget

The **My Picture** option (see Figure 5.4) in the General Settings allows you to select a photograph that will be displayed to other Gmail users with whom you make contact. You can choose if it will be visible to everyone or just to those with whom you exchange e-mail or chat messages. Your picture will appear to them when they scroll over your name in their Inbox (see Figure 4.3), Contacts, Chat list, or even when someone looks at your public Google Profile.

You can show or hide the **People Widget** in your General Settings. Choose **Show the people widget** if you want information about the people who send you e-mail messages to appear on the right hand column of their message. You need to click on their name (on the right side of the message they send to you) to view information about your contact. (See Figure 4.4 to see how the message looks if you have selected to show the People Widget.) The information comes from various sources, such as your contact manager (which might contain the contact's name, e-mail address, or occupation). Also included on the right column are lists of recent Google+ posts, e-mail messages, thumbnails of photos your contact has sent you, and any Google Calendar events or documents your contact has shared with you.

The People Widget also gives you the ability to initiate a Chat or Hangout session or send an e-mail, among other actions (see Lesson 9 for more details). After clicking the **Show details** link at the bottom of the People Widget, additional recent e-mail, documents, or other interactions between you and the individual will be displayed (see Figure 4.4; The **Show details** link is not displayed in Figure 4.4 because we already clicked it.).

Create Contacts for Auto-Complete

Although you can import contacts from other e-mail software (e.g., Outlook) into Gmail, you can also have Gmail add a contact every time you send a message to a new person. These people are assigned the **Other** label in your contacts. The next time you compose an e-mail to that person, as you begin typing their name into the **To** line, their e-mail address will appear in a drop-down list for you to select. If you don't like this option, you can select **I'll add contacts myself**.

See Lesson 7 for information on how to import/export contacts and add contacts using Gmail's Contact Manager.

Vacation Responder

Before you go on vacation, you can set a **Vacation Responder** so an automatic reply is sent to anyone who e-mails you (this is the default) or just to people in your Contacts who send you an e-mail, or only to people in your company (e.g., *Internet for Lawyers* shown in Figure 5.3). So as not

Figure 5.3 Vacation Responder

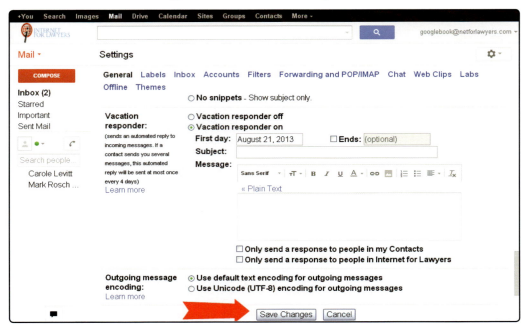

to annoy people who e-mail you multiple times when you are on vacation, the vacation responder won't send the same person an automatic reply every time (not more than once every four days).

Personal Level Indicator

The **Personal level indicator** option allows you to show (or not show) one chevron (to the left of the subject line) to indicate a message was sent to your e-mail address, among others (e.g., you are cc'd, but the message is not from a mailing list) or two chevrons to indicate a message was sent only to your e-mail address.

Snippets

The **Snippets** option allows you to choose whether to display the text previews of messages as shown in Figure 2.1 or only the subject line.

Stars

Stars (and other symbols) are another way to categorize and organize your messages. There are no meanings pre-assigned to any of the stars or symbols because they are primarily useful for people who respond better to visual cues than to text cues and symbols (such as Labels) (see Figure 5.4). Previously, Gmail offered only a yellow star, but has now expanded the stars to five other colors and added six others for you to use to mark messages. Drag the stars/symbols from the **Not in use** area to the **In use** area. As you view your list of messages, each time you click on a star it will change colors until you find the one you want to mark a particular message with.

Figure 5.4 Stars

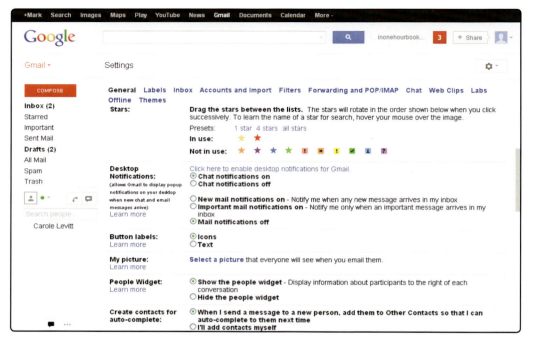

Labs Settings: Add Experimental Features, Gadgets, and Functions to Gmail

Some of the most useful Gmail features offers are its experimental Labs capabilities, where Google allows you to add additional tools to your Gmail Inbox interface (see Figure 5.5). Google periodically creates new add-on tools for Gmail, and these experimental features are made available to users by selecting the **Labs** tab from the **Settings** (see Figure 5.5). Clicking the **Enable** button next to any experimental Labs project adds that feature to your Gmail account—but not until you click **Save Changes** at the bottom of the page. For some of the Labs projects, you also need to go to the **General** tab and make further selections. (For an example, see the discussion about the **Undo Send** lab project on page 38). To turn off a feature, return to the **Labs** tab and click **Disable.**

Sample Labs

There are many Labs to choose from, but we'll just highlight a few of our favorites, such as **Canned Responses**, the **Google Calendar** gadget, the **Undo Send** capability, the **Google Docs** gadget, and **Google Docs previews in mail**.

> **USAGE TIP**
>
> Remember that these are experimental features that Google describes as not "quite ready for primetime," and that they "may change, break or disappear at any time." While we have not had any major issues with the Labs we've enabled, Google does offer an "escape hatch" in the event that a Labs feature malfunctions and keeps your Gmail Inbox from loading properly. Use this URL to open your Inbox without loading any of your enabled Labs: https://mail.google.com/mail/u/0/?labs=0.

Figure 5.5 Labs

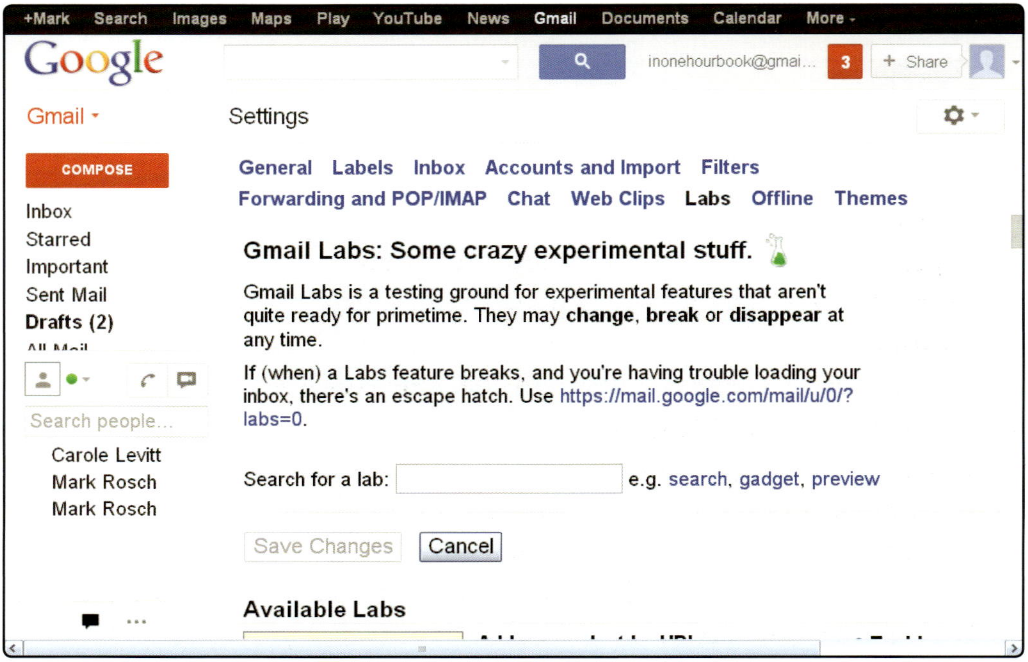

Undo Send

Both authors have added the **Undo Send** labs feature. If you have ever sent an e-mail message and regretted it immediately after hitting the send button or realized that the message you just sent was addressed to the wrong "Mike" from your contact list, then this is the feature for you. Go to your **Settings**, choose **Labs**, and then choose **Enable** from the **Undo Send** lab option (see Figure 5.6a). After selecting Undo Send from the Labs, you need to visit the **General** tab and select 5, 10, 20, or 30 seconds from the **Send Cancellation period** drop-down list and then click **Save Changes**. From this point forward, after you click the send button on any Gmail message, you get a chance to undo (unsend) the message. Even though the message at the top of the message list says " Your message has been sent" it really hasn't been sent . . . yet. The **Undo Send** Labs experiment gives you a small window of time in which to pull the message back, as if you never clicked the **Send** button (see Figure 5.6b).

Figure 5.6a Undo Send Settings

Figure 5.6b Undo a Sent Message

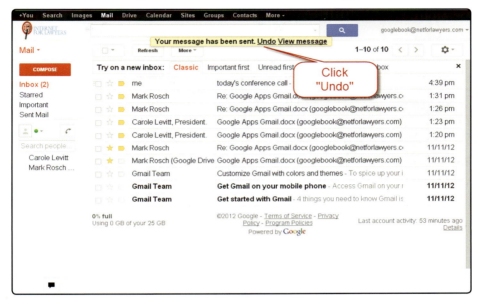

Clicking the **Undo** link pulls the message from your outbox and places it in your **Drafts** folder, unlike the "Recall Message" feature in Microsoft's Outlook, which is not actually able to recall the message, in most instances. Instead, Outlook draws even more attention to the message you initially sent by sending the recipient a new message announcing that you want to recall the first message. In Gmail, the recipient gets no notification that anything was sent or recalled/undone.

Canned Responses

Do you send the same e-mail messages frequently? Now you can stop hunting for that earlier response to an e-mail to copy and paste it into a new e-mail to send to a different person who asked the same question. Go to your **Settings**, choose **Labs**, and then choose **Enable** from the **Canned Responses** lab option. Remember to click **Save Changes**.

To create a new **Canned Response**, see Figure 5.7 and follow these steps:

1. Type your text into the message window.
2. Click the unlabeled down-arrow (if you hover, the words **More Options** will appear) in the lower right-hand corner of the message. A pop-up will appear.
3. From the pop-up, click **Canned Responses**.
4. A new pop-up will appear. Select **New canned response** from the list.
5. A dialog box will appear asking you to name the new canned response. Enter a name, and click **okay**. Now you are ready to insert the e-mail address and subject and send the message.
6. When you want to insert any of your canned responses into an e-mail, repeat steps 2 and 3, and select the canned response that you want to insert from the **Insert** section of the drop-down list.
7. Canned Responses can be deleted by using steps 2 and 3 and then selecting the canned response that you want to delete from the **Delete** section of the drop-down list.

> **PRACTICE TIP**
>
> "About a year ago, we received a bunch of inquiries from our website for a mass tort," said said Clayton Hasbrook, an associate at the Oklahoma City firm of Hasbrook and Hasbrook. "I used the Canned Responses feature a lot to reply to those people."

Lesson 5 Settings 41

Figure 5.7 Canned Response

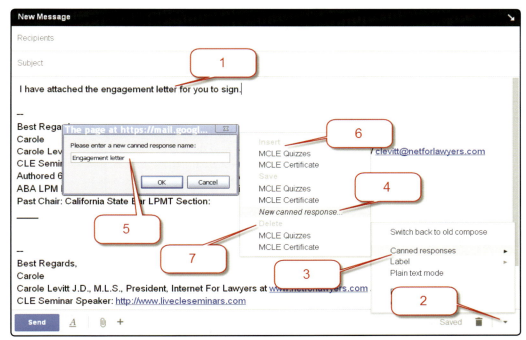

Google Calendar and Google Docs Gadget

To display information from your Calendar and a few recent Google Docs in the left-hand column of your Gmail Web interface, go to **Settings**, choose **Labs**, and then choose **Enable** for the **Google Docs gadget** and the **Google Calendar gadget**. Remember to click **Save Changes**.

To view these two gadgets in your Inbox (see Figure 5.8), hover over the ellipsis found at the bottom of the Inbox's left-hand column. The word **Gadgets** will appear, which you need to click to view your calendar and documents.

42 Google Gmail and Calendar in One Hour for Lawyers

Figure 5.8 Calendar and Docs Gadgets

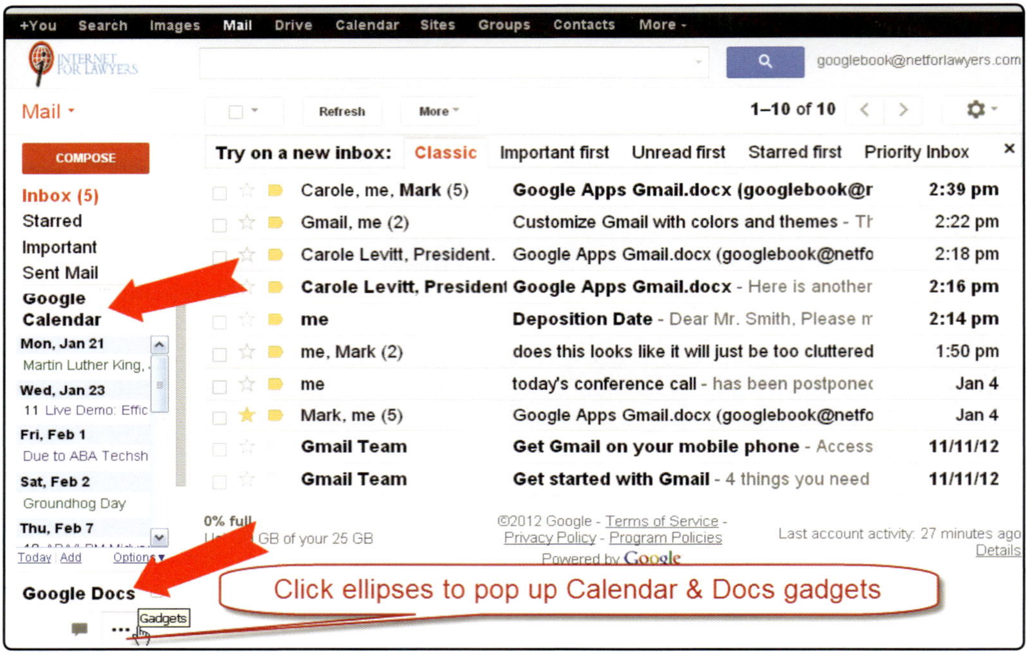

Google Docs Previews in Mail

When someone sends you e-mail with a link to a Google document, spreadsheet, or presentation, you can open the full document directly in Google Docs (without downloading the document) if you have enabled the **Google Docs previews in mail** lab option. To enable this lab option, go to **Settings**, choose **Labs**, and then choose **Enable** for **Google Docs previews in mail**. Remember to click **Save Changes**. Once enabled, just click **View** at the bottom of any received e-mail.

Accounts Settings

The Accounts Settings tab allows you to further customize how you send, receive, grant access to others to handle your e-mails, and process messages in your Gmail account. You can also use this setting to change your account password.

Figure 5.9 Accounts Settings

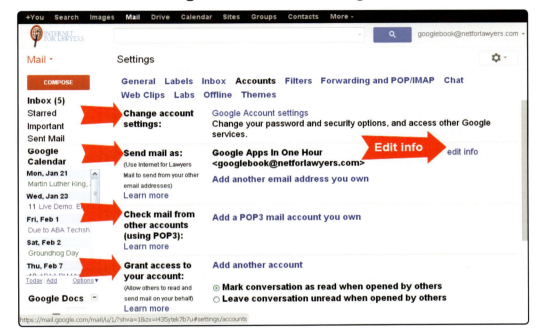

Check Mail from Other Accounts

Use the **Check mail from other accounts [using POP3]** option from the **Accounts** setting to receive all messages from up to five other (non-Gmail) e-mail accounts in your one Gmail account (see Figure 5.9). This can be useful if you choose to retain these other non-Gmail accounts and not import them into Gmail. If you have an old, generic e-mail address that you've distributed to many people or appears in Yellow Pages advertising, this is much easier than trying to get the word out that you've changed your e-mail address.

To separate these e-mails, you can create Filters to assign discrete Custom Labels to messages that come from each of your other e-mail accounts. For example, Mark is able to receive e-mails in his Gmail Inbox sent to his mrosch@mindspring.com, mrosch@netforlawyers.com, and mrosch@earthlink.net addresses. This way, he only has to check one e-mail inbox. He has also created individual Filters and corresponding Custom Labels so that, when a message is addressed to mrosch@mindspring.com, it bypasses the Gmail Inbox and is automatically assigned the Mindspring Custom Label that he created for this purpose.

See page 49 for more information about creating Filters.

> **PRACTICE TIP**
>
> You can use this setting to configure your work Google Apps e-mail Inbox to also retrieve messages from your personal e-mail address(es). This way you do not have to switch back and forth between accounts to be sure that you receive important personal messages.

> **USAGE TIP**
>
> The **edit info** link on the right-hand side of the **Send mail as** section (see Figure 5.9) is used to change the identifier associated with your outgoing Gmail messages (e.g., instead of just *Mark Rosch*, Mark could change this to *Mark Rosch, Vice President*). Be sure to type the entire name and designation (*Vice-President*) into the editing box. For example, Mark could not just type "*Vice President*" into the editing box. He must type *Mark Rosch, Vice President.*

Send Mail As

When you send messages from your Gmail account, but you want the From line to display one of your other e-mail addresses, you can do this with the **Send Mail As** setting (see Figure 5.9).

This option allows you to send messages via the Gmail web interface that are listed as coming **From** those other e-mail accounts you own. For example, Mark's Google Apps for Business Gmail address is mrosch@netforlawyers.com, but he also owns mrosch@earthlink.net and mrosch@mindspring.com. As described in the previous section, he prefers to receive messages from all of those accounts in his mrosch@netforlawyers.com Inbox. Utilizing the **Send mail as** setting, he is able to send messages "from" any one of those accounts after receiving them in his mrosch@netforlawyers.com Gmail Inbox, as described below.

To set up this feature, click **Add another e-mail address you own** and type another of your e-mail addresses. (Repeat this step to add additional addresses.) To send a message from any of the addresses you've added, click the **From** link that appears next to your e-mail address when you compose your message. After clicking **From**, a drop-down menu appears. From there, you can select the e-mail address you prefer to send from. (If you're replying to a message or forwarding a message instead of composing a new message, you need to click into the area where the recipients are listed and then click **From**.)

> **USAGE TIP**
>
> When using the **Send Mail As** feature, be sure to select the **Send through [your e-mail provider's] servers** option during the setup process. This minimizes the possibility of your messages getting caught in the recipient's Spam filter.

Grant Access to Your Account

When you're out of the office on vacation, or even at a meeting or appearance, it can be helpful to delegate someone else (e.g., your secretary or paralegal) to have access to your Gmail account to check for important messages or to draft long e-mail replies. Some people do this today by sharing their login information and password—which raises extraordinary security and ethical issues. But Gmail lets you do this without sharing your password by delegating authority—indefinitely or temporarily—using the **Grant access to your account** option (see Figure 5.9). The other person will be able to check your e-mails and respond for you when necessary. This only works if the other person also has a Gmail account, and of course you'll need to provide Google with the Gmail address of each person to whom you are granting access.

> ### USAGE TIP
>
> The practice of sharing passwords to delegate access to an e-mail account would qualify as a "worst practices" benchmark. And it happens far too frequently because e-mail providers have not—until recently—made some form of controlled delegation part of their offerings. Specifically, while you might trust a colleague or employee to read your e-mail and respond on your behalf for a week or two, or even on an ongoing basis, sharing your password is an entirely different matter. If you use that same password or a derivative of that password on other systems (e.g., banking, Amazon, or PayPal), then you are opening a door to financial risks that are extraordinary. And in today's IT environment, with the increasing prevalence of Single Sign On (in which signing into one account automatically signs you into other accounts), giving out your e-mail password might be giving out access to other files—including performance evaluations, salary information or highly-sensitive client data. This can't be stressed enough: If you want to delegate privileged access to your e-mail, you should choose a system that offers controlled delegation—like Google Apps for Business or Microsoft Exchange—and you should use it. Especially in a law office, there is no excuse for sharing passwords.

Additionally, you can enable one of these options: **Mark conversation as read when opened by others** or **Leave conversation unread when opened by others**.

Forwarding and POP/IMAP Settings: Accessing Gmail Messages from Other E-mail Accounts or Software

As discussed in Lesson 2, Gmail allows you to retrieve your Gmail messages using your favorite e-mail software (including Microsoft Outlook, Thunderbird, Eudora, and Apple Mail) instead of using Gmail's web-based interface. This is what Carole does.

There are a few different ways to achieve this. Rather than just forwarding messages from one account to another, we recommend configuring your account to authorize your favorite e-mail software to access the Gmail servers directly to download your messages using one of two mail transfer protocols—**POP** or **IMAP**.

POP Download

POP is most-commonly used in small office environments, so we describe the process for using it here. To receive Gmail messages in your favorite e-mail software, you must go to **Settings**, choose the **Forwarding and POP/IMAP** tab and **Enable POP for all mail** in Gmail's **POP Download** section (see Figure 5.10). If you want to stop receiving Gmail messages in your favorite e-mail software, you can **Disable POP**. You can also use the drop-down menu in the **When messages are accessed with POP** section to instruct Gmail how to handle messages (on Gmail's own servers) once you have downloaded those messages to your e-mail software. You can select from **keep [e-mail sender's] copy in the inbox**, **archive [e-mail sender's] copy**, or **delete [e-mail sender's] copy**. (See Lesson 19 for a link to detailed configuration instructions.)

Figure 5.10 Forwarding and POP/IMAP Settings

IMAP Access

IMAP Access (see Figure 5.10) allows you to access messages similar to the way you can if you enable POP. IMAP Access offers greater synchronizing capabilities between the Gmail settings and your e-mail software. Because of IMAP's two-way synchronization, enabling IMAP access can be a useful way to migrate your existing e-mail messages (and folders) from Outlook to the Gmail web interface.

If you prefer to use IMAP, the customization options on the **Forwarding and POP/IMAP** tab are similar to those described for POP Access. Google also offers detailed instructions for configuring IMAP access via your e-mail software at http://linkon.in/N5GMEK.

If you're not certain whether you prefer POP or IMAP access, Google has a descriptive page that outlines the benefits of each method at http://linkon.in/N5Grlr.

Forwarding Messages in Gmail

Gmail will forward all of your incoming messages to another e-mail account you own if you select **Add a forwarding address** (see Figure 5.10) and designate another e-mail address to which the messages should be sent. You can also use the drop-down menu (next to the e-mail address box) to instruct Gmail how to handle messages (on Gmail's own servers) after they've been forwarded. The options on this drop-down menu are the same as the drop-down menu in the **POP Download** section (as described on page 47).

Additionally, you can forward selective e-mails by creating a filter to identify specific e-mail characteristics (e.g., keywords in the message body or subject line, from particular people) and selecting the **Forward it to** option in the set-up menu. (See below for more details about creating filters.)

Filters Settings: Creating Filters to Manage the E-mail Messages You Receive

Similar to Outlook and other e-mail software, Gmail allows you to set up **Filters** to automatically categorize/sort your messages as they are received. (In Outlook, this feature is called Rules.) Click the **Filters** tab in **Settings** and then the **Create a new filter** link to initiate the process of creating a new filter to organize your incoming messages (see Figure 5.11a). You can even export filters from one Gmail account to import into another Gmail account. In the example in Figure 5.11b, we type the word word *TECHSHOW* into the **Has the words** box, and then we click **Create filter with this search** (see Figure 5.11b).

Figure 5.11a–b Create a New Filter

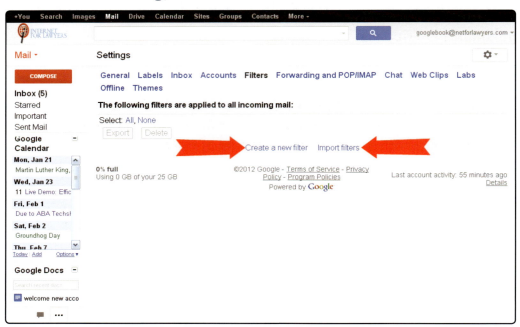

Lesson 5 Settings **51**

> **PRACTICE TIP**
>
> "My main advice for lawyers, with whatever e-mail service they're using, is to filter e-mail messages into folders," said Clayton Hasbrook, an associate at the Oklahoma City firm of Hasbrook and Hasbrook. "All listservs should be filtered, that's a given," he continued, "but we receive incoming faxes via e-mail (each fax goes to everyone's e-mail) and I like having those inbound faxes go to a designated folder. For me, the faxes 'skip the inbox,'" he explained. "My paralegal wants to be able to see them in her Inbox, and she can do that. We did label a folder for her called '1 Inbound Fax' so that folder will be first in the list of folders. So she can look at the inbound faxes in the Inbox or in that fax folder."

After you click **Create filter with this search**, a pop-up box is displayed for you to tell Gmail what to do with the messages you want filtered: **Skip the Inbox (Archive it)** (places messages in the All Mail folder), **Mark as read**, **Star it**, **Apply the label** (that you select from the drop-down menu), **Forward it to** (the e-mail address you designate; see the previous Lesson for more details on forwarding), **Delete it**, **Never send it to Spam**, **Send canned response: Choose canned response**, **Always mark it as important**, or **Never mark it as important**. You can apply this filter to all previously received messages currently stored in this Gmail account that include the keyword *TECHSHOW* anywhere in the message by checking off **Also apply filter to x matching conversations** (where x is the number of conversations returned by the search for the word *TECHSHOW*).

52 Google Gmail and Calendar in One Hour for Lawyers

> **PRACTICE TIP**
>
> "Beyond the basic operations of create, read and search, the most important tools for managing big volumes of e-mail are folders, labels and filtering," says G. Burgess Allison, Information Technology Director, MITRE Corporation. "The analogy I tell to lawyers of a certain generation is that filters handle your e-mail the way a first-rate legal assistant handles your snail mail. Filters organize the routine e-mails that they can recognize, highlight the e-mails that are most important, and narrow down the number of uncategorized e-mails that need to be read and at least scanned immediately."

Exporting and Importing Filters

Filters can be exported and imported to be shared among different accounts or users (see Figure 5.12) especially the sophisticated filters you create for particular clients or matters.

To select a Filter (or Filters) to export, first click the **Filters** tab in **Settings** (see Figure 5.11a) to display all the Filters you have created. Then click into the checkbox(es) next to the Filter(s) you want to export and click the **Export** button (see Figure 5.12). A pop-up window then prompts you to navigate to a location on your hard drive in which to save the Filter(s) and to give that file a name (see Figure 5.12). Clicking the **Save** button in the pop-up window saves the Filter(s) to your hard drive.

> **USAGE TIP**
>
> To share the filters with your colleagues, attach the file to an e-mail for them to download and import. Also, if you have multiple Gmail accounts you can use these functions to share your filters between them.

Figure 5.12 Exporting Filters

To import a Filter, click the **Import Filters** link (shown on Figure 5.11a) and then the **Choose File** button to locate the file on your computer. When you locate the Filter file, click **Open File** and then **Create Filters**. However, if you want to **Apply new filters to existing email**, click the check box to the left of that choice before you click **Create Filters**. You can edit or delete any of your Filters by visiting the **Settings' Filters** tab.

Web Clips Setting

By default, Gmail places Web Clips (ads and/or news and information) from outside sources into a bar above your list of received messages and also above each message that you open in Gmail's web-based interface.

Free Gmail and free Google Apps accounts include both ads and news and information in this space, while paid Google Apps for Business accounts only display news and information in this space. Regardless of the type of account you have, if you prefer not to see any of this information, you can turn the Web Clips off entirely (see Figure 5.13). Removing the Web Clips from the top of your Inbox is as easy as unchecking the box marked **Show my web clips above the inbox** on the **Web Clips** settings tab.

Google used to allow you to customize your Web Clips in Gmail with information from sources you selected, but due to low usage Google removed this capability and Google now places random information in the Web Clips. For this reason, we recommend turning them off.

Figure 5.13 Disable Web Clips

Lesson 6

Searching the Full Text of Messages

Like most of Google's services, Gmail offers both a simple search (accessed by typing search terms into the box at the top of the Gmail Web interface (see Figure 6.1a)) and a set of more advanced search features (see Figure 6.1b) hidden behind the unmarked down-arrow on the right-hand side of the simple search box (see Figure 6.1a). If you hover over the down-arrow, a **Show search option** notation pops up. (The change to **Show search option** link used to be prominently displayed to the right of the search box. It's a crime that Google has chosen to hide such a useful tool. Don't forget to look for it and use it.)

Figure 6.1a Simple Search Options

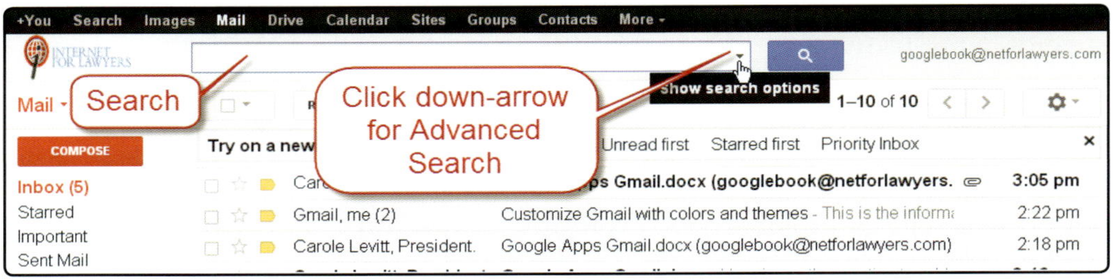

55

Figure 6.1b Advanced Search Options

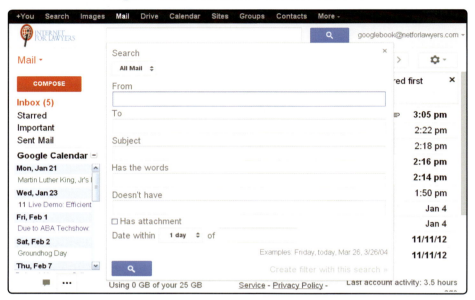

Gmail's advanced **Search options** menu allows you to full-text search your Gmail messages by including and excluding keywords. You can search through **All Mail** (note that the **All Mail** search does not include messages labeled **Trash** or **Spam**), limit the search to mail stored in specific folders (such as **Trash** or **Follow up**), or limit results to **Read Mail** or **Unread Mail**. Searches can also be restricted to messages: **To** or **From** a specific individual, that have **Attachments**, or include specific **Subject** line. You can limit your search results to messages sent or received during a specific time frame (e.g., **Date within**).

Beyond the targeted search options available on the advanced search box, Google also makes a long list of other Gmail search limiters available at http://linkon.in/REhqui. One of the most useful is **in:anywhere:**, which will search all Messages, even Spam and Trash. For instance you could search *in:anywhere:"negligence per se"* to locate e-mails with that exact phrase in *all* of your mail. Note that phrase searching and Boolean connectors can all be employed when creating a search.

Lesson 7

Contacts and Tasks Manager

Gmail also has an integrated Contact and Task Manager. To access them, click on the down-arrow to the right of the red **Mail** (this could say **Gmail** if you are using a free account), located at the top of the Inbox's left-hand column (see Figure 7.1). Use the drop-down arrow to the right of the Mail button in the upper left-hand corner of the Inbox to navigate between the Inbox and the **Contacts** and **Tasks** managers.

Figure 7.1 Contacts and Tasks

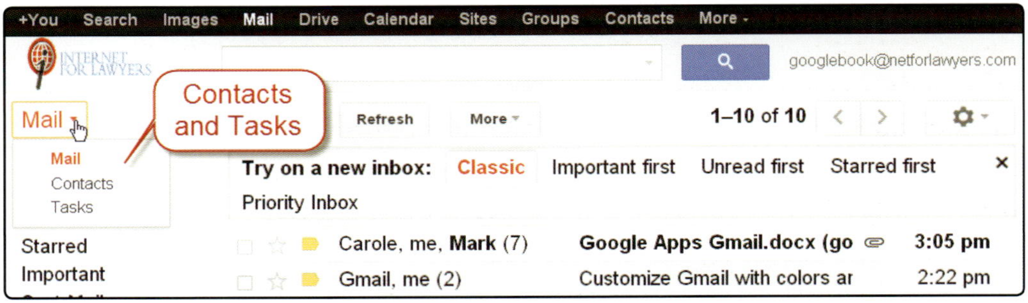

Contacts Manager

You can import contacts from other e-mail software (Outlook, Outlook Express, Thunderbird, Yahoo! Mail, Hotmail, Eudora, and others) using a CSV file and via vCard from apps such as Apple's Address Book (for detailed instructions, see http://linkon.in/OMwHcq). You can also enter individuals into the contact list one at a time. Alternately, you can rely on Gmail's default list of contacts automatically created from e-mail addresses with whom Gmail detects you frequently correspond (see Figure 7.3).

Add New Contacts Manually

After you select **Contacts** from the drop-down list shown in Figure 7.1, a **New Contact** button appears on the left-hand side (see Figure 7.2). If you click that, an **Add Name** menu appears in the middle while other choices appear in the left-hand column, such as **New Group** and **Import Contacts**. Clicking **Add Name** allows you to type the contact's name directly into that space. You can also add a picture of your contact on this same screen by clicking on **Add a picture** to the left of **Add Name**. If you hover over, a pop-up appears with fields in which to enter more detailed information, such as the **Prefix**; **Suffix**; and **First**, **Middle**, and **Last** names. Other drop-down lists appear if you hover over **E-mail**, **Work Phone**, **Mobile Phone**, or **Address**. For instance, after clicking **Work Phone** or **Mobile Phone**, you can add nine different types of numbers, from home, to Google Voice, to fax, etc.

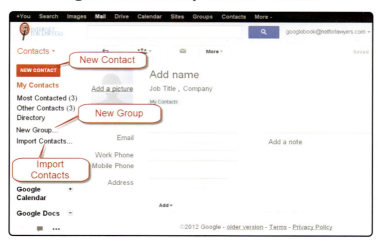

Figure 7.2 Manually Add New Contact

Lesson 7 Contacts and Tasks Manager   59

In Figure 7.2, notice the **Add a Note** box to the right where you can add additional information about the contact. Clicking the **Add** button (beneath the **Address**) displays a drop-down menu allowing you to enter additional information such as a **Nickname**, a **Company/Title**, or any **Custom** field that you can define. When you are done adding a new contact, the information is automatically saved.

Add Other Contacts to My Contacts

Google automatically assembles a default list of **Other Contacts** based on e-mail messages you send and receive. To add any of Gmail's default Other Contacts to **My Contacts**, click **Other Contacts** in the left-hand column (as seen in Figure 7.3). After reviewing the Other Contacts list, click to add a checkmark to the box to the left of each contact you would like to add and then click **Add to My Contacts**. To add all of the Other Contacts, simply use the pull-down arrow to the right of the unlabeled box that is to the left of **Add to My Contacts** and select **All**. The **More**

Figure 7.3 Add to Contacts

drop-down menu allows you to manage these contacts. For example, you can **Print** them, **Sort by First Name** or **Last Name**, or **Restore contacts** that you had previously deleted (you can choose the time span, from 10 minutes ago up to the past 30 days).

Creating Groups of Contacts

Gmail also allows you to create groups of multiple contacts so you can send e-mails to all members of that group simply by typing the group's name into the message's **To** box.

To create a group, select **New group** from the drop-down menu in the left column (as seen in Figure 7.2) and type a name for your group.

To add existing contacts to a group, click the checkbox to the left of any name you want to add, click the Groups button located above **My Contacts** (the icon looks like a group of three people). Click the drop-down arrow, and select an existing group from the drop-down menu and then click **Apply**. In the alternative, you can click **Create new** to create a new Group from here to add the contact to.

Tasks Manager

Gmail also has an integrated Tasks Manager that allows you to list and track tasks. You can access it by clicking the **Tasks** link on the drop-down menu, in the left-hand column of the Inbox (as shown in Figure 7.1).

> **USAGE TIP**
>
> Tasks added to your **Tasks** list are stored in a Tasks calendar that can also be accessed/displayed with any Calendars you create. (See the *Create Multiple Calendars* Practice Tip at the beginning of Lesson 12 for more information.)

Lesson 7 Contacts and Tasks Manager

The first time you create a Tasks list, its name is automatically generated from your e-mail address (ours is "Google Apps in One Hour's List" as shown in Figure 7.4c). However, you can **Rename** any list, **Delete a List** or create a **New list** by clicking on the **Menu** icon (the last icon in the lower right-hand corner as shown in Figure 7.4a). Notice the black bar in Figure 7.4a, which shows that we created a new **Tasks** list with the name, "Brown matter." Clicking into the checkbox next to any task places lines through the task, indicating it has been completed (see the first task in Figure 7.4a).

Type a new task into the space to the right of the check box and then click the right-pointing chevron that appears next to the task to Edit details (see Figure 7.4a).

Figure 7.4a Create New Task

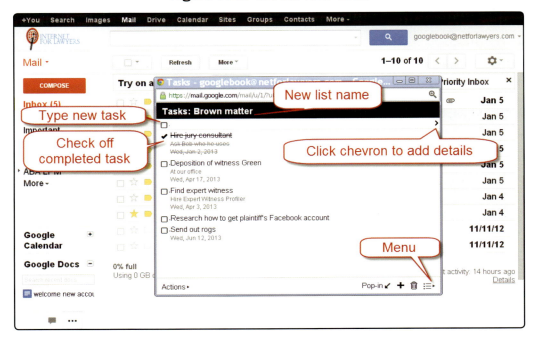

62   Google Gmail and Calendar in One Hour for Lawyers

With the **Edit details** menu (see Figure 7.4b), you can add a **Due date** and notes to describe a task. Clicking the "**+**" adds a new task to the list. Clicking the **Trash can** icon deletes a selected task.

Figure 7.4b Add Task Details

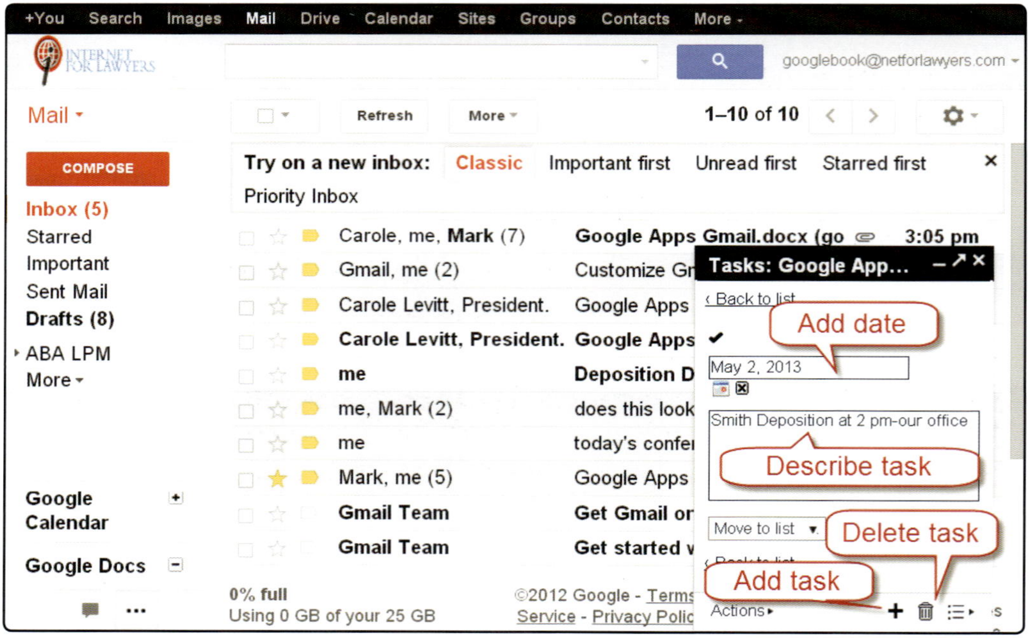

From the **Edit Details** menu (see Figure 7.4c), you can do the following:

1. Go back to the list (**Back to list**).
2. Move a task to another list (**Move to list**).
3. Click the **Actions** menu in the lower left-hand corner of the **Tasks** list to manipulate the tasks and the list (e.g., tasks can be moved up or down and the list can be sorted by due date, printed, or e-mailed). You can also view all past completed tasks or clear the list of completed tasks. Detailed **Help** and usage tips can also be accessed from this **Actions** menu.

Figure 7.4c Task Edit Details Menu

> **PRACTICE TIP**
>
> Some attorneys create separate task lists for certain clients or matters. Other attorneys prefer to create separate calendars for certain clients or matters, instead. (See the Create Multiple Calendars Practice Tip at the beginning of Lesson 12 for more information.)

Lesson 8

Offline Access to Your Gmail Messages

One concern many people have about using an online storage system for their e-mail messages is the inability to access those messages in the absence of an Internet connection. Gmail solves this problem by giving you offline access to your messages even when you're not connected to the Internet. The Offline feature is only available if you're using Google's Chrome web browser. For that reason, it makes sense to install Chrome even if just for this one purpose.

To use Gmail in offline mode, you'll need the free Offline Gmail helper plug-in for Chrome. It can be downloaded and installed at http://linkon.in/pE7TvA. After the plug-in is installed on your computer, you need to open a new tab in your Google Chrome web browser while connected to the Internet (see Figure 8.1a).

Clicking the blue **Offline Gmail icon** launches the application and opens a new browser window that prompts you to **Allow offline mail** (see Figure 8.1b). Selecting **Allow offline mail** and clicking **Continue** automatically downloads a collection of messages to be available offline. The Gmail Offline Inbox looks different from the desktop Gmail browser-based interface, but it similar to the Gmail mobile web browser interface (see Figure 8.1c).

Figure 8.1a–c Gmail Offline

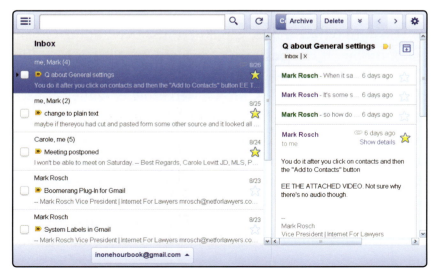

From here on out, any time you're not connected to the Internet and you launch the Gmail Offline app in your Chrome web browser, it gives you access to the most recently downloaded messages, allowing you to view, compose, reply, and so on to those messages. The next time you connect to the Internet and open Gmail in your Chrome browser, the changes you made to those messages will be synchronized and any new messages you've written will be sent.

Lesson 9

Google Chat/Google Talk and Google Hangout

Like the better-known free Skype service, **Google Chat/Google Talk** is Google's free text, voice, and video-chat instant-messaging service. It is available to anyone with a Google account. **Chat** and **Talk** are basically the same, except that **Chat** runs in a web browser and **Talk** is a stand-alone application. To run **Google Chat** in a browser, you'll use the Google Voice and Video Chat browser plug-in that integrates Google Chat into Gmail (and also into Google+ and some other Google services). If you don't want to use the browser, then you can run the stand-alone Google Talk application that you download and install on your computer.

The Google Voice and Video Chat browser plug-in is available for the operating systems Windows, Linux, and Mac OS X 10.4 and newer. The stand-alone Google Talk application is available only for Windows XP and newer. Both Chat and Talk can be downloaded at http://www.google.com/talk/.

Google Chat and Talk do not involve telephones. Each party is using their computer's microphone to speak. However, Google does offer a service that allows one party to use their computer to place a call to the other party's telephone (See Lesson 10 to learn about **Call Phone**).

70 Google Gmail and Calendar in One Hour for Lawyers

> **USAGE TIP**
>
> You must have both a microphone and a camera built into or connected to your computer in order to use the combined audio and video features of Google Chat or Google Talk. Without a microphone and camera, you could still use just the instant messaging features to send text-based messages. If you have a microphone, but no camera, then you could at least use Google **Chat** or **Talk** to talk to each other via your computer. If you do not have a camera but you do have a microphone, then you will be able to voice chat.

To this point, our book has primarily covered accessing Google services through the web browser, so this section focuses on the first method of using Google Chat—through the web browser plug-in, via Gmail. We also focus on the web browser method because it works on a larger number of operating systems than the stand-alone application (as noted earlier).

In the late summer of 2012, Google integrated the **Hangout** multi-user video chat feature from its Google+ social network into Google Chat. Therefore, some of Google Chat's on-screen instructions refer to Hangout rather than Video Chat. The primary difference between these two is that Video Chat is one-to-one and Hangouts are one-to-many. Hangouts can include you and up to nine other (invited) participants, or can even be opened up to anyone (up to nine besides you) on the web as a Hangout On Air broadcast.

> **PRACTICE TIP**
>
> Google Chat and Talk can be useful for quick real-time one-to-one video conferences between members of your firm, clients, co-counsel, etc. For quick real-time video conferences with up to 10 people, use Hangouts.

Google Chat/Talk Settings

After you install either the Google Voice and Video Chat plug-in or the stand-alone Google Talk application, access its settings by clicking the

Gear Icon button in the upper right-hand corner of the Gmail Inbox. On the drop-down menu, click the **Settings** option, then click the **Chat** tab.

Setting Up Your Camera, Microphone, and Speakers

Use the **Camera**, **Microphone**, and **Speakers** drop-down menus to select the devices on your computer to use for the audio and video chat. Obviously, you should test your audio/video equipment before you use Chat/Talk for the first time. Links and tools in the **Verify your settings** section help you determine whether your devices are working with the Google Talk plug-in (see Figure 9.1). If you're having hardware issues, click the **Troubleshoot your settings** link to try to diagnose the problem.

Figure 9.1 Chat Settings

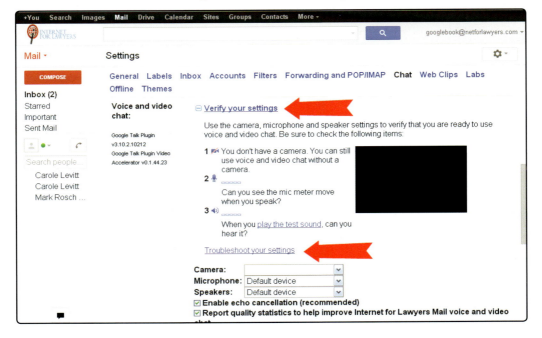

Reporting Chat/Talk Statistics Back to Google

The **Report quality statistics to help improve [your account name] voice and video** (see the last line in Figure 9.1) sends non-identifiable information about connection quality and so on back to Google.

> **PRACTICE TIP**
>
> Many security advocates prefer not to allow this outbound flow of information from their networks. It is probably a good idea to un-check this box.

Saving Transcripts of Text Chats

In the **Chat** settings tab, Google Chat gives you the option of saving the transcripts of your text chats (instant messaging) to your Gmail account. (A Chats label is created.) Note that this feature relates only to text chats and does not create a transcript of the dialogue of your video or voice chats.

> **USAGE TIP**
>
> Saved chats are an extremely useful feature because your text chats can then be searched and retrieved like e-mail messages using the web-based interface.

You can customize how Google Chat stores transcripts of your text chats in the **My Chat History** section of the Chat settings tab (see Figure 9.2). On the **Chat** settings tab you can opt to **Save chat history** or **Never save chat history**. Note that even if you are saving your chat history, you can stop recording any chat by selecting **Off the record** from the chat conversation **More** menu (see Figure 9.6b). Note,

> **PRACTICE TIP**
>
> Once you start using and saving text chats with your colleagues, you'll find that they can replace e-mails in certain instances because the transcripts can contain instructions, links, and other information that you can later retrieve.

Figure 9.2 Chat History

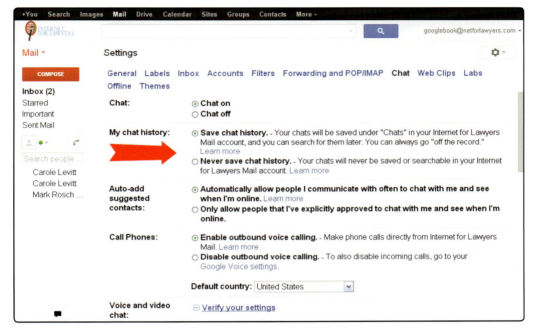

too, that once you take a chat conversation with someone "off the record," all future chat conversations with that same individual are off the record until you unselect that option. Be aware that even if you have taken a chat Off the Record, the person with whom you are chatting might still have the capability of capturing and storing the content of the chat if they are saving the chat history on their end.

Starting with Google Chat/Talk

After you install the browser plug-in on your computer, a small green camera icon appears next to your name profile picture (if you have not inserted a picture, then you will only see a silhouette) in the Chat gadget of the left-hand column of your Gmail Inbox (see Figure 9.3). If the Chat gadget does not automatically appear in the left-hand column of

Figure 9.3 Chat Gadget

your Inbox, click the "talk bubble" icon 🗨 at the bottom of that column to open it. Clicking the down-arrow next to your profile photo allows you to set your availability to chat as **Available**, **Busy**, or a custom message, as well as customize the look of the Chat gadget in your browser.

Before you can start chatting with other Gmail users, you must invite them to chat by hovering over their name in the left-hand column of your Gmail Inbox (a pop-out, as shown in Figure 9.4, will then appear to the right). You can click the smaller **Invite to chat** icon in the lower right hand corner of the pop-out window to chat (see Figure 9.4). Ignore the large **Add and invite** button unless you want to add this person to one of your Google+ Circles. (Circles are people you've placed into one or more groups with whom you interact via Google's social networking feature, Google+). The people you invite to one of your Circles must also accept the invitation before you can actually add them to your Circle.

Figure 9.4 Invite to Chat

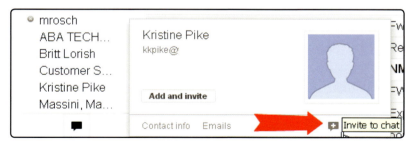

Once you begin using Google Chat, you will also see a green icon next to the names of Contacts from whom you have previously accepted invitations to chat (or vice versa) if they are currently online and available (Google Chat-enabled). The icon might be a green ball (if you last text chatted with the person) or a green camera (if you last video chatted or participated in a Hangout with that person). Similarly, those people will see the same icon next to your name in their Gmail Inbox, indicating that you're Google Chat-enabled.

Initiating a Google Text Chat, One to-One Video Chat, or Voice Chat
By Hovering Over a Contact

Hovering over any of the chat-enabled **Contact** names in the **Chat** section of the left-hand column of your Gmail Inbox pops up a window with additional information about that person, including their e-mail address, and any Circles (e.g., **Family**) you have added them to (see Figure 9.5 where author Mark Rosch is using his Gmail account and displaying

Figure 9.5 Displaying Contact Details

author Carole Levitt's contact details). Clicking on the **Contact info** link opens that person's full record in your Contacts. Clicking the **E-mails** link displays recent e-mails with this contact. A series of buttons appears in the lower right-hand corner of the pop-up window. Depending on your past interaction with that contact they will differ. The buttons allow you to **start a Hangout**, or start a text **Chat with this Contact**, **e-mail this contact**, or **Call this contact** (this initiates a voice chat session using each of your computers' microphones to talk, rather than the **Call Phone** service as described in Lesson 10 where you use your computer to call the other person's mobile or landline telephone).

If Person is Online, Initiate Chat By Clicking On Their Name

If you notice that one of your contacts is online, instead of hovering over their name, you can instead click on their **Contact** name from the list to begin a text message by beginning to type into the text box that has the smiling face in Figure 9.6a. You can also begin a hangout or a one-to-one voice chat (it will say **Voice Calling**, which means using your computer to call the other party's computer and you will each be speaking through your microphones) by clicking the corresponding icon/button in the upper left-hand corner of the active chat window that pops up (see Figure 9.6a).

Figures 9.6a–b Additional Contact Details

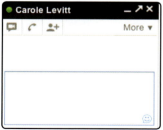 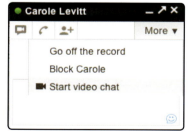

The third button in Figures 9.6a and b ⊶ in the upper left-hand corner gives you the option to invite additional contacts to the chat. The upward-pointing arrow (in the upper-right hand corner of the chat window) invokes the pop-out option that moves the chat to its own browser window if you prefer a larger space (see Figure 9.6b). Clicking the **More** drop-down menu in either Figure 9.6a or 9.6b gives you the ability to begin a video chat just with this particular Contact, as opposed to a multi-user Hangout. See page 72 for more information about the **Go off the record** option found behind the **More** drop-down menu.

> **USAGE TIP**
>
> In addition to conducting chat sessions using your computer, you can conduct chat sessions on the go in the web browser of your iPhone or iPad (or with Google Talk apps for Android and Blackberry phones). There are even rumors that Google is developing 3-D video chat technology for mobile devices.

Lesson 10

Call Phone: Telephone Calls from Within Gmail

For the last two to three years, Google has been famously integrating its various products and services. One example is the ability to place calls to landline and mobile telephones using your computer and the Gmail Inbox in your web browser. With a strong Internet connection and a headset, the voice quality rivals that of cell phone or landline connections.

After you install the Google Chat plug-in for your web browser (discussed in Lesson 9), the Chat gadget is added to the left-hand column of your Gmail Inbox. At the top of the Chat gadget on the left-hand side of Figure 9.5 just to the right of the camera icon, a Phone button appears.

Clicking the **Call Phone** button opens a pop-up keypad (see Figure 10.1) that allows users in the United States and Canada to call any landline or mobile phone in the United States or Canada for free. Rates for calls to other countries vary, but start as low as $.02 per minute. From the drop-down menu in the upper-right hand corner you can access the **Rates** link. This is one instance where an advanced Google service does not require the other person to also be using Google.

> **PRACTICE TIP**
>
> Because these Google Talk calls use your Internet connection and don't require you to use a landline or cell phone, they can be a useful alternative for those instances where you have no cell phone service but are able to connect to a Wi-Fi network. Note that you will want to have headphones so nobody else can hear the person on the other end of the call. Be aware that your end of the conversation would be easy to overhear, which could lead to a breach of confidentiality. While there are special headsets and earphones with built-in mics made to be used with these kind of calls, regular earbuds, where you'd still be using your laptop's built-in mic, would do in a pinch.

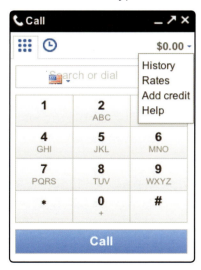

Figure 10.1 Pop-up Phone Keypad

When calling, click the flag icon in the **Search or dial** box. Type the phone number into the **Search or dial** box and press the **Call** button to place the call. You can also type a name into the **Search or dial** box to search through your Contacts. If the contact record for a particular person includes a phone number, it appears and you can click it to place the call.

Lesson 11

Migrating Existing E-mail Messages to Gmail

In Lesson 5, we discussed ways to receive your Gmail messages in your favorite e-mail client, such as Microsoft Outlook. But, if you prefer to move entirely to the Gmail web-based interface that we describe in this book, Google provides a desktop utility to help make that change. The Google Apps Migration for Microsoft Outlook's (GAMMO's) step-by-step wizard assists you in moving your existing e-mail messages, calendar items, and personal contacts from Outlook to your Google Apps account. The ability to migrate data from Outlook to Gmail is only available for Windows.

> **USAGE TIP**
>
> GAMMO is particularly useful in multi-user firms where some users want to stick with Outlook and others want to move to Google's web-based interface, because each user can choose to migrate his or her e-mail, contacts, and calendar data from Microsoft Outlook profiles and PST files to Google Apps . . . or not.

Migrating your messages is a multi-step process. The first step must be taken by your domain Administrator (if you're a solo attorney, this might be you), and the subsequent steps must be taken by you.

> **USAGE TIP**
>
> While this book is generally meant as a step-by-step guide for those implementing Google Gmail and Calendar, we also recognize that there are those who prefer to work with a consultant to get the ball rolling. For those people, Google has created a network of Authorized Resellers who must successfully convert a minimum number of users and pass a written exam (among other milestones) before gaining certification. A search for Google Apps Resellers will return a long list of these vendors.

Step 1: Administrator Must Enable E-mail Migration

Before you can use the GAMMO tool, your Google Apps domain Administrator (See Lesson 10) must enable the e-mail migration option in the Google Apps Administrator's control panel. The Administrator must go to the **Settings** tab, select the **e-mail** option in the left-hand column and then, on the **General** sub-tab, scroll all the way down to the **User e-mail uploads** section. If the administrator checks **Allow users to upload mail using the e-mail Migration API,** you will be allowed to use the GAMMO tool. Note that this migration is only available to paid Google Apps for Business accounts, not free Google Apps accounts.

Step 2: User Downloads and Installs GAMMO

Download the GAMMO application at https://tools.google.com/dlpage/outlookmigration and install it on your computer. It is compatible with Windows XP (and newer) and Outlook 2003 (and newer).

Run GAMMO to Migrate E-mail Messages from Outlook to Gmail

Once installed, double click the **GAMMO application** on your hard drive to begin the process of moving information from Outlook to Gmail.

In the GAMMO application's first step in migrating your information to Google's web-based interface, you select the **Outlook profile** (Exchange servers only) or **PST** (Personal Storage Table) **file**, which contains the e-mail messages and other data you want to migrate to Gmail.

> **USAGE TIP**
>
> In Windows 7 and 8, the PST file can usually be found in the following location on your computer: <drive>:\Users\<user>\AppData\Local\Microsoft\Outlook.
> In Windows XP, it is usually stored in the following location on your computer: <drive>:\Documents and Settings\<user>\Local Settings\Application Data\Microsoft\Outlook.

In the second step of the migration process, you can select which of your personal data you want to migrate, including **e-mail messages**, **Contacts**, and the items in your **Calendar**. You can also set a date range for the e-mail messages you want to migrate (see Figure 11.1), and decide whether or not you want to move your **Deleted items** or **Junk mail**.

Figure 11.1 GAMMO Step 2

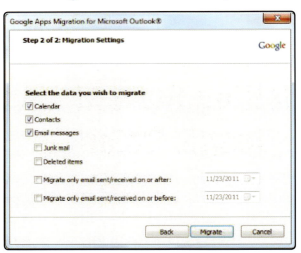

Clicking the **Migrate** button automatically completes the process based on the choices you make in these two steps.

Lesson 12

Getting Started with Google Calendar

After you log into your Google account, click on the **Calendar** link in the top black bar to display your calendar (see Figure 12.1). You can also reach your calendar at http://calendar.google.com. Google Calendar is a

Figure 12.1 General Calendar View

full-featured appointment calendar. You can add appointments, events, reminders, etc., and access them from anywhere you have an Internet connection (or even without an Internet connection—see Lesson 18), including web-enabled cellular phones.

> **PRACTICE TIP**
>
> **Create Multiple Calendars**
>
> You can create separate Google Calendars to list professional and personal events, engagements, etc. You can set the default privacy setting for a particular calendar as public or private, and you can control whether individual events on a calendar are public or private. You can even create a separate private calendar to share with a client. Each can be managed separately.
>
> The names of those Calendars appear on the left-hand side of the Calendar interface (e.g., **Carole Levitt, Internet For Lawyers, Tasks, Travel** in Figure 12.1). Clicking on the name of any of the individual Calendars adds it to or removes it from the display you're viewing in your browser.

You can sync your Google Calendar with stand-alone products such as Microsoft Outlook, Apple iCal, and Mozilla Sunbird using the free tools available at http://www.google.com/sync/, or you can export your existing calendar events from one of these calendars to the Google Calendar web interface we discuss in this Lesson. (See Lesson 11 for information on migrating calendar events from Microsoft Outlook.)

One advantage Google Calendar gives you over stand-alone calendar products is the ability to view and edit your calendar from any computer or mobile device with an Internet connection and the ability to share your calendar with others on the Internet. As with Gmail, however, you can also store your Google Calendar information on your own hard drive to access your events and appointments when you do not have an Internet connection (see Lesson 18).

Because Google Calendar is integrated with the rest of the services in Google Apps, you can also access other Google functions, such as the Tasks list (discussed in Lesson 7).

> **USAGE TIP**
>
> You can also add extended features via the **Labs** tab in your Calendar's **Settings**. For example, you can attach any of your Google Docs to an event (see Lesson 17 for more details on this and other experimental features).

Figure 12.2 displays the one-month view of the authors' public Google Calendar, showing our events and appointments. Using the buttons on the upper right-hand side of the screen, you can select different views of your calendar, including the **Day**, **Week**, **Month**, or **Agenda** view. In between the **Month** and **Agenda** buttons, notice the **5 Days** button. This is the only button that allows you to customize the view from **2 days** through **7 days**. Through the **General Tab** in **Settings** (click the **Gear Icon** in the upper right-hand corner to reach **Settings**), you can choose to view anywhere from 2 through 7 days, or **2 weeks**, or **3 weeks**, or **4 weeks**.

When you are in the month view, you can quickly scroll through the months by using the left arrows or right arrows next to the Today button (see Figure 12.2). If you are in the Day or Week view, these arrows move to the next day or next week (respectively). Using the left arrows or right arrows above the smaller calendar in the far left-hand column moves only that calendar and not the larger one.

88 Google Gmail and Calendar in One Hour for Lawyers

Figure 12.2

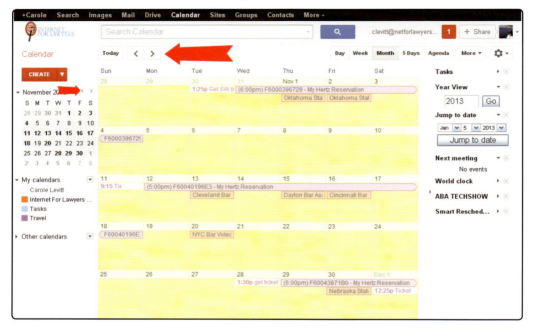

Lesson 13

Adding Events to Google Calendar

There are three ways to add new events to your Google Calendar:

1. Click the red **Create** button in the left-hand column (see Figure 12.2), which gives the most options for entering information about your event/appointment.

2. Use the **Quick Add** by clicking the down arrow to the right of the red **Create** button.

3. Click into any date and time on the calendar.

> **PRACTICE TIP**
>
> An event could be a deposition, a trial date, a client pitch meeting, or a conference.

Creating Events with the Create Button

Clicking the **Create** button in the left-hand column opens an event menu, which gives you the ability to enter a large amount of information about your event/appointment (see Figure 13.1a). You can enter an event name (**Untitled event** box), beginning and ending times, location (**Where**), and a **Description**. You can schedule a multi-person video conference by clicking the **Add a Google+ Hangout** link. (See Lesson 9 for more information about Hangouts.)

Figures 13.1a–b Calendar Events and Invitations

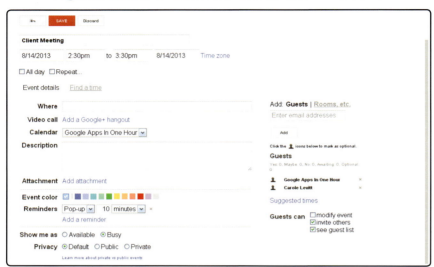

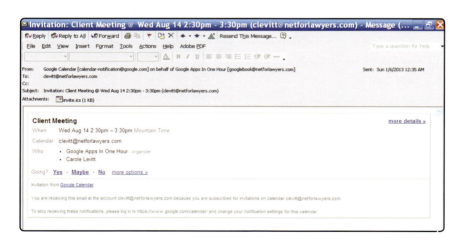

Use the **Add guests** box on the right-hand side of the event menu to invite other guests to the event. Figure 13.1b illustrates how an invitation to the event created in Figure 13.1a, using Google Calendar, appears as an e-mail viewed in Microsoft Outlook. Clicking the **Find a time** tab allows you to better coordinate the invitations to the new event on your Google Calendar

Lesson 13 Adding Events to Google Calendar **91**

with the schedules of other Google Calendar users whom you invite to the event (and whose calendars you have access to). You can also set reminders to **E-mail** you or open a **Pop-up** on your computer at set times (**weeks**, **days**, **hours**, or **minutes** before the event).

You can set the **Privacy** level of individual events on your calendar as **Public** or **Private**. You can set the access to individual events to be more or less strict than the default setting of the calendar you're adding the event to. If you enable the **Event Attachment** lab (see Lesson 17 for more details about this **Labs** feature), you can also use the **Add Attachment** link to add documents from your computer or your Google Drive to the event listing. Note that if you attach a document from Google Drive, you must also share it with people you invite to the event or they will not be able to view the document.

PRACTICE TIP

If you travel, it's important to click the **Time zone** link to include that information about your event. Google Calendar is "time zone aware" and can automatically adjust any events on your Calendar to the time in your current time zone (see Lesson 17). This can be helpful, for example, if you enter the time for a conference call to take place in one week at 3 p.m. Mountain Time, but on the day of that conference call, you happen to be in Los Angeles, on Pacific time. Google would automatically change the time on the event to read one hour earlier to adjust for the difference in time zones—and you wouldn't miss the call.

92 Google Gmail and Calendar in One Hour for Lawyers

Creating Events with the Quick Add Box

The **Quick Add** button is hidden behind an unmarked drop-down arrow to the right of the Create button. Clicking this drop-down arrow opens the Quick Add dialog box (see figure 13.2). You can enter the event/appointment (e.g., *Smith interrogatories due*) and add a fixed date (e.g., *11/21*) or you can use a relative date as illustrated here (e.g., *next Wednesday*). Google understands both. Clicking the **Add** button (or your computer's **Enter** key) adds the event/appointment to your calendar.

Figure 13.2 Finding the Quick Add button

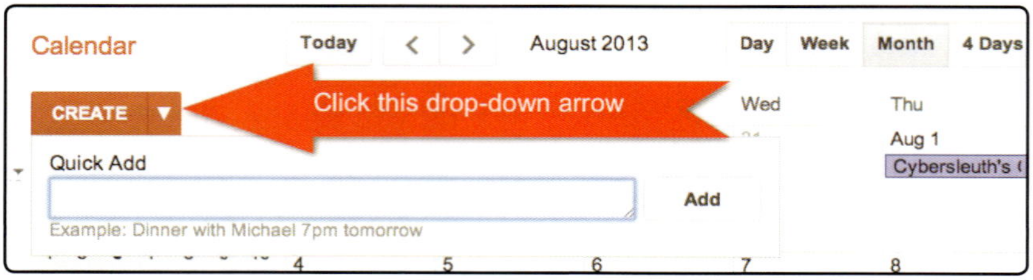

USAGE TIP

Help Your Guests Or Clients Find Your Events

Adding an address to the **Where** information allows Google Calendar to generate a link to a Google Map for the event's location.

Creating Events by Clicking into the Calendar

You can also create a new event by clicking into any date on your calendar (see Figure 13.3). Like using the Quick Add box, this method only allows you to enter minimal information about the event you're creating [e.g., title and time (**What**)]. Clicking the **Create event** link adds the event to your Calendar. Clicking the **Edit event** button allows you to add additional information about the event and to invite guests, as discussed above.

Figure 13.3 Add Events Directly to Calendar

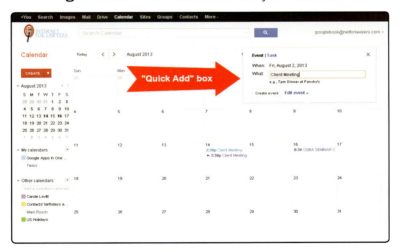

In addition to adding a new Event to your Calendar by clicking into any date, you can also add a new **Task** to your Task Manager by clicking the **Task** link at the top of the pop-up window that appears after you click into any date on your Calendar. See Lesson 7 to learn about Tasks.

Lesson 14

Editing Events You've Added to the Calendar

Events can be edited after they have been added to the Calendar. First, click on the event in the Calendar (see Figure 14.1a). Next, click the **Edit event** link that appears in the lower right-hand corner of the subsequent pop-up window. The event creation screen (see Figure 13.1a), where you can change any of the event information (e.g., **Where**, **Description**, **Time**), appears.

Figure 14.1a Editing Calendar Events

Figure 14.1b More Actions for Calendar Events

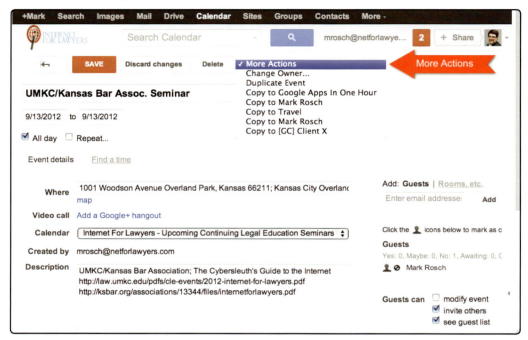

The **More Actions** drop-down menu (see Figure 14.1b) lets you **Duplicate** (an) **event** (and assign a different date to the duplicate), copy the event to one of your other Calendars, or transfer ownership of the event (**Change Owner**) to another Google Calendar user—even one outside of your firm. Note however that if ownership of an event is transferred, the event then appears on the new owner's Calendar and disappears from yours. (The new owner would have to invite you to the event for it to reappear in your Calendar.)

Be sure to click the **Save** button on the top left-hand side of the screen before leaving this page. The unmarked arrow button to the left of the Save button takes you back to your full Calendar (not pictured in Figure 14.1b).

Lesson 15

Searching for Events and Appointments in Your Google Calendar

Another advantage of Google Calendar is its ability to easily search and retrieve messages. Like most of Google's services, Calendar offers both a "simple" search (accessed by typing search terms into the **Search Calendar** box at the top of the Calendar Web interface) and a set of more advanced search features. Google Calendar hides this Advanced Search menu behind an unlabeled drop-down arrow on the right-hand side of its search box (see Figure 15.1).

Figure 15.1 Advanced Search Location

Google Calendar's advanced **Search Options** menu allows you to search through your calendar events and appointments for keywords and phrases in **What** (event names), **Who** (specific invited individuals), and **Where** (specific locations) fields to target your search results. Additionally, if you have more than one Google Calendar (e.g., one personal and one professional), you can expand your search to **All Calendars** or focus on just one of them. You can also limit your search results by excluding words (**Doesn't have**) to appointments set during a date range (**Date**) (see Figure 15.2).

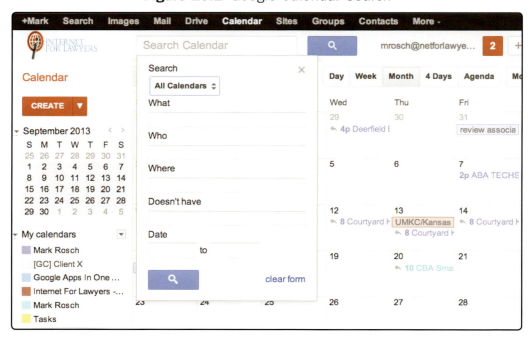

Figure 15.2 Google Calendar Search

Lesson 16

Printing Your Calendar

Google gives you the ability to print portions of your Calendar. Unfortunately, you cannot customize the information that is printed.

Use the **Print** option found on the **More** drop-down menu on the upper right-hand side of the Calendar interface to print a paper copy of the view of the Calendar you're currently using (e.g., Day, Week, Month, Agenda). The print copy includes just the calendars that are selected to display on the screen (see Figure 16.1).

Using the Print option on the More drop-down menu opens a **Calendar Print Preview** pop-up window, where you can set some of the parameters for the information to be included in the printed page(s) (see Figure 16.1). The pop-up offers different options depending on which view of the Calendar you're currently using (as illustrated in the next section).

Figure 16.1 Print Calendar

Printing the Calendar Agenda View

The **Agenda** view offers the most printing options. When using this view of your Calendar, you can opt to:

- **Print descriptions**
- **Print end times**
- **Print attendees**
- **Print your response**
- **Show events you have declined**
- [print in] **Black and white**

In the **Agenda** view, the **Calendar Print Preview** window (see Figure 16.2) allows you to customize the **Print** [date] **Range**, **Font size**, and **Orientation** (e.g., **Portrait**, **Landscape**, **Auto**). But when printing from other views, the Calendar Print Preview window offers only the Print Range, Font size, Orientation, Show events you have declined, and Black and white options. Clicking the **Print** button opens a new window in which you can select the printer you want to use to print your Calendar. Clicking the **Save As . . .** button opens a new window in which you can opt to save the document as a PDF on your computer.

Figure 16.2 Calendar Print Preview

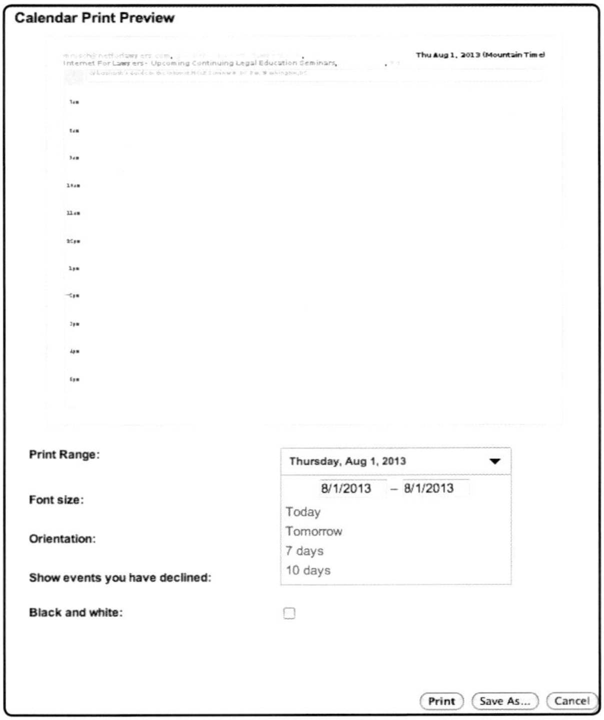

What Actually Prints When You Select Print

Clicking the **Print** option from the **More** drop-down menu sends the exact view of events in your Web browser to be printed (see Figure 16.1). While you can adjust the date range and some other parameters (depending on the view of the Calendar you're using) in the Calendar Print Preview window, we think it would also be useful to be able to add other Calendars from our list to the printout while in the Preview window.

All printed versions generated by the Calendar include some information that we think is unnecessary in a paper copy. For example, the individual names of each one of your Calendars that's included in the printout is listed at the top of the page. Additionally, the name of the creator of each event is listed in printouts of the Agenda view. We think it would be more useful in many instances to be able to eliminate these two extra pieces of information from the printout.

Lesson 17

Customizing Your Calendar with Settings

Like Gmail, Google Calendar offers a collection of settings to customize the display of information in the calendar. You can access them by clicking the **Gear Icon** in the upper right-hand corner of the Inbox.

Setting Your Time Zone Using Google Calendar's General Settings Tab

Most of the settings on the **General** Settings tab are self-explanatory. You can select your preferred **Time format**, **Date format**, etc., on this tab.

The **Current Time Zone** setting is a little trickier though. Because Google Calendar is "time zone aware," it sometimes automatically detects that you are not in your Calendar's

> **PRACTICE TIP**
>
> We keep a travel calendar with all of our flight times. The default time zone for that calendar is Mountain Time, so any flight added to the calendar is assumed to be in Mountain Time. If we have a 2:30 p.m. departure from New York City, we must assign the Eastern time zone to that flight, otherwise the calendar automatically assumes it to be in Mountain Time.

104 Google Gmail and Calendar in One Hour for Lawyers

default time zone and adjusts any events to the time in your current time zone. You can also set your Current Time Zone manually on this tab. However, if you have not assigned a Time Zone to your events, as discussed in the Practice Tips on page 87 and page 99, this could make incorrect times appear on your calendar—which would not be helpful when checking for your departure time, for instance.

Sharing Your Calendar Using Google Calendar's Calendars Settings Tab

The **Calendars** Settings tab is where you can control how and with whom you share your entire Calendar (e.g., you might share your calendar with your secretary, practice group, or even a client if you set up an individual calendar for a specific client). If you have created more than one calendar, you will see them all listed here. Clicking any of the individual Calendars brings up the next three tabs discussed below.

> **PRACTICE TIP**
>
> The Dayton, Ohio-based Burton Law firm uses shared Google Calendars for its lawyers and staff. Firm Principal Chad Burton appreciates "the ease of viewing co-workers' calendars and scheduling group meetings or other events."

Calendar Details Tab

The **Calendar Details** tab is where you give your calendar a **Calendar Name** and **Description** (see Figure 17.1). From this tab, you can also generate HTML code so you can **Embed This Calendar** into your existing website, if you choose to have a public calendar (e.g., for speaking engagements).

Lesson 17 Customizing Your Calendar with Settings   **105**

You can also click any of the buttons in the **Calendar Address** section of the Calendar Details tab to get a web address that you can share with others to access the public events on your Calendar. The **XML** button generates code for the RSS feed of events in the calendar. This feed can be used to add calendar information to any web page. For public Calendars, you can add a **Description** and a **Location** to help people locate your calendar in search engine searches.

Figure 17.1 Calendar Details

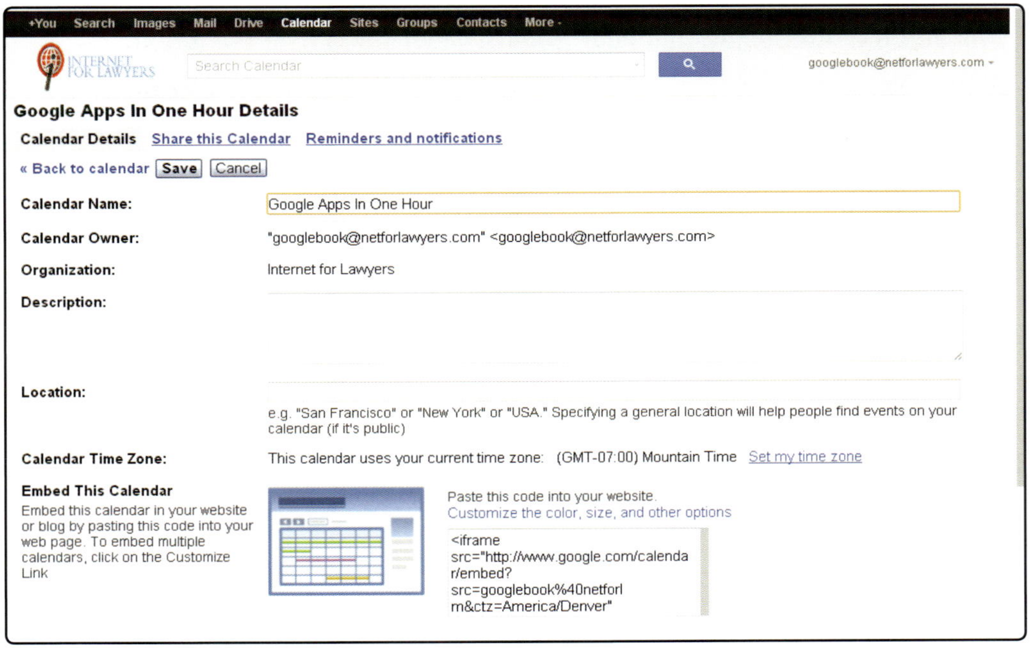

> **USAGE EXAMPLE**
>
> ### Embedding Google Calendar in an Existing Web Site
>
> We have been using Google Calendar to share our schedule of live MCLE seminars around the country since 2004. By using Google Calendar, we can update information on upcoming events in one place and have it automatically update in other places on the Web.
>
> For example, if you visit our website (http://www.netforlawyers.com), on the left-hand side of the home page you will see XML data from our calendar's RSS feed integrated into the first column (about one-third of the way down the page). Additionally, if you click the **Calendar** link on our site you will see the full Google Calendar (**Month** view) containing our seminars. We have even added Google Calendar information to our Facebook profiles.

Clicking any of the buttons in the **Private Address** section generates a web address that will show anyone to whom you send this link all of the events—public and private—on your calendar. Note that if you inadvertently share the private address with someone who you wish that you hadn't, you can click the **Reset private URLs** link to invalidate all previous private addresses you've generated.

Share this Calendar Tab

On the **Share this Calendar** tab, you can indicate whether you want all Internet users to be able to see your Calendar, or just other registered users of your domain's Google Apps account (e.g., anyone in your firm). You can also give specific people rights to view or post events to the Calendar (even those outside your firm). You can assign specific individuals access to your calendar to **Make changes AND manage sharing**, **Make changes to events**, **See all event details**, or **See only free/busy (hide details)** by entering their e-mail address in the **Enter e-mail address** box, selecting one of the access options from the drop-down menu, and clicking the **Add person** button (see Figure 17.2).

Lesson 17 Customizing Your Calendar with Settings   **107**

Figure 17.2 Calendar-Sharing Options

Calendar Reminders and Notifications Tab

If you have authorized multiple people (e.g., your secretary, paralegal, or other lawyers at your firm) to post and edit events on the calendar, you can use the **Reminders and Notifications** tab (as seen in Figure 17.3) to opt into notifications by e-mail or SMS (text) message from the calendar of new or changed events, or cancelled invitations. On the Reminders and Notifications tab, you can also request the calendar to send you an e-mail with your **Daily agenda** each morning at 5:00 a.m. local time.

Figure 17.3 Calendar Notifications

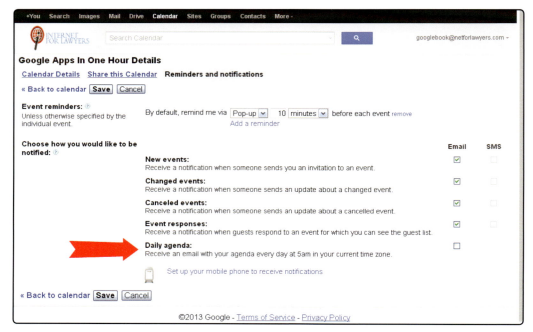

Calendar Mobile Setup Tab

Google Calendar can be configured to send alerts about upcoming events and appointments via text messages to your cellular phone. Google does not charge for this feature, but your regular phone company rates for receiving text messages apply.

To do so, enter your **Phone number** in the box on the Calendar **Mobile Setup** tab and then click the **Send Verification Code** button. You will then receive a **Verification Code** via text message to the number you entered. Return to this tab to enter that code in the Verification Code box and click **Finish setup** to complete the configuration. The feature works with most major U.S. and Canadian cellular carriers, but it does not work with pre-paid phones. A complete list of compatible phone companies is available at http://support.google.com/calendar/bin/answer.py?hl=en&answer=37226&ctx=tltp.

Calendar Labs Tab

Google development teams and other engineers periodically create new add-on tools for Google Calendar. Note that Google describes these Labs as "a testing ground for experimental features that aren't quite ready for primetime. They may change, break or disappear at any time." However, we have not had any noticeable issues when using them.

These experimental add-ons are available behind the **Labs** settings tab. To access this tab, the Labs feature must be enabled in the Administrator's Control Panel (see Lesson 19).

Simply click the **Enable** button next to any of the Labs experiments you want to add to your Calendar, and then scroll to the bottom of the page and click the **Save** button. Three useful Labs experiments for Calendars are:

- **Event Attachments**, which allows you to attach documents to your event listings
- **Jump to date**, which allows you to go directly to any date on your Calendar (rather than clicking on the month/year and then selecting the day from the grid)
- **Smart Rescheduler**, which helps you see the availability of others in your firm who you want to schedule meetings with (this feature only works if the other people have shared their Google Calendar with you)

Lesson 18

Accessing Google Calendar Without an Internet Connection

Like Gmail, one concern many people have about using a web-based calendar is the inability to access it in the absence of an Internet connection. Google Calendar solves this problem by giving you offline access to your calendar even when you're not connected to the Internet. (The offline version of the Calendar looks similar to the online version.)

The offline feature is only available with the addition of the free Google Calendar helper application available for the Google Chrome web browser. It can be downloaded and installed at http://linkon.in/RP2jCD. (Note that the plug-in is *not* available for the Chrome browser on mobile devices.) After the plug-in is installed on your computer, you will need to open a new tab in your Google Chrome web browser while connected to the Internet to begin enabling the plug-in and saving information from your Calendar onto your computer.

Once the plug-in is installed, you still have to enable it to download your calendar information. To do so, open your **Calendar**, click the **Gear Icon** in the upper right-hand corner of the Inbox, and select **Offline** from the drop-down menu. This opens the pop-up window seen in Figure 18.1a. Check the **Available Offline** box (shown in Figure 18.1b) next to

Figures 18.1a–b Offline Calendar Window and Tab

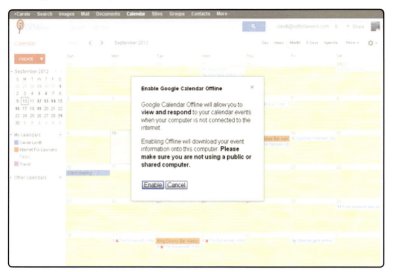

each of the Calendars you want to be downloaded and then click the **Save** button. A green spinning circle next to a calendar indicates information is still downloading. A green check mark next to a calendar indicates information has been downloaded. After you complete this step, you can revisit the Offline selection on the drop-down menu to determine if all of your Calendar information has downloaded.

Depending on the number of events in your Calendar(s), the plug-in downloads approximately two months worth of events, beginning about two weeks before the current date and running about six weeks after. When initially enabled, however, the plug-in only downloads information from your primary Calendar. In order to include additional Calendars, you must visit the (newly added by the plug-in) Offline Settings tab. (For more information about accessing the Settings, see Lesson 17.)

Once the plug-in is installed and enabled and you have selected all of the Calendars you want to include, you will be able to view and RSVP to invitations when your computer is not connected to the Internet. You will not be able to add new events or edit existing ones until you are back online.

> **USAGE TIP**
>
> You can have access to all of your calendar events on your mobile device(s)—with or without an Internet connection—by syncing your online Google calendar with those devices as discussed at the beginning of Lesson 12.

Lesson 19

Dashboard

In the Introduction, we said that, "this book is not intended to be an implementation guide for IT professionals." However, any solo attorney or small firm who opts to replace its traditional, installed office productivity suite with Google Apps will need to designate at least one person to manage and customize the various aspects of the firm's Google Apps account by accessing the account Administrator's dashboard. This usually falls to the "techie" at the firm. If you're reading this lesson, it's probably you.

The following sections don't necessarily discuss every setting available on each tab, but rather focus on the ones most likely to be of interest to law firms getting familiar with their **Google Apps for Business Accounts**.

> **USAGE TIP**
>
> To verify and activate your Google Apps account, it is necessary to access either your domain name registration, your web-hosting account, or both. If you are unsure who your domain registrar or web-hosting company is, or are unsure how to access these accounts (or even what a server is), it may be wise to contact whomever built your website or the customer service department at your registrar (or web-hosting company) to see if someone can help you through this part of the process.

Signing Up for Your Google Apps Account

To create your Google Apps for Business Account, go to https://www.google.com/a/signup/ and follow the steps of the registration process. As of this writing, there is a thirty-day free trial available. You are not asked for a credit card during registration process, and you can cancel your account at any point during the trial and incur no charges.

Also during the registration process, you are asked to create your first user's account. Pick a user name that will serve as the e-mail address for that account (e.g., mrosch@netforlawyers.com).

Verifying that You Own Your Domain

Before allowing you to send and receive e-mails, etc., from a domain you've registered, Google wants to verify that you are in fact the owner of that domain. Google offers four different verification methods to do this.

The recommended method is the **Domain Name Provider** method, which requires you to log into your account with the company where you registered your domain name (e.g., GoDaddy, Network Solutions). Google has verification tools/instructions for nearly three dozen of the most popular domain name registrars.

You can also opt to verify your domain by:

- **The HTML Tag Method.** Add an HTML meta-tag provided by Google to your site's home page.
- **The HTML File Upload Method.** Upload an HTML file provided by Google to the Web server hosting your site.
- **Connecting Your Accounts.** Connect your Google Apps for Business account to your existing Google Analytics account.

Setting Up Your Google Apps Account

Once you've verified your domain, Google provides a useful setup wizard that will walk you through the steps necessary to configure the apps in your account. You can access it by clicking the **Setup** tab at the top of the Administrator's Control Panel, which can be reached via a link in the confirming e-mail you receive from Google. (Later, the Administrator's Control panel can be reached from the Gmail Web Inbox by clicking the **Gear Icon** on the upper right-hand side of the browser window and selecting the **Manage this domain** option on the subsequent drop-down list.)

The **Express** wizard is described as "best for small organizations." It would probably meet the needs of most solo attorneys or small firms. There is also a **Custom** wizard for more advanced implementations.

Adding Users

To add users to your account, click the **Users and Groups** tab on the left-hand side of the **Custom** wizard (see Figure 19.1), then the **Add Users** sub-tab, and then follow the directions in the center panel of the browser window. Remember that each user you create will eventually be billed to you at the rate of $50 per year.

Figure 19.1 Users and Groups Tab

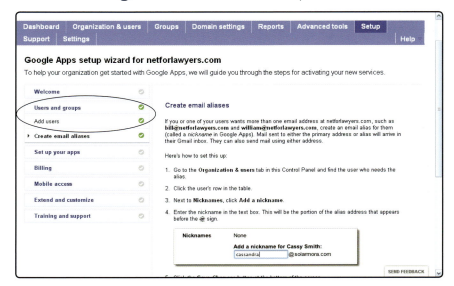

You can also use the **Create e-mail aliases** sub-tab to create alternate or secondary e-mail addresses for your users without having to pay for another user (see Figure 19.1). For example, if someone at the firm has a name that's often misspelled (e.g., Allen) you might want to create two e-mail addresses for that person: one with the correct spelling *allen@netforlawyers.com* and an alias with the common misspelling *alan@netforlawyers.com*. Using the **Create e-mail aliases** sub-tab, we can create that secondary e-mail address for our user *Allen* at no extra charge.

> **PRACTICE TIP**
>
> "I like that Google Apps lets us set up multiple aliases for each user," said Clayton Hasbrook, an associate at the Oklahoma City firm of Hasbrook and Hasbrook, "so I can have clay@hasbrooklaw.com, cth@hasbrooklaw.com, and clayton@hasbrooklaw.com all go to the same inbox."

> **USAGE TIP**
>
> You can also add additional users or create **Nicknames** for existing users after the initial setup by clicking the **Organization & Users** tab on the Administrator's dashboard.

Updating Your Mail Exchanger Records

The most important part of the Gmail setup involves changing the Mail Exchanger (MX) records for your domain to point to Google's mail servers. It's very important that you only do this *after* you have created accounts for all of your users, as described in the previous Section.

Updating your Mail Exchanger records requires you to log into your account with the company where you registered your domain name (e.g., GoDaddy, Network Solutions) to make the change. Google offers specific instructions to configure the MX records in nearly three dozen of the most popular domain name registrars, as well as more generic instructions that can be used at any registrar not on Google's list. Note that if your website is hosted with a different company than you registered your domain with, you might have to log into your web-hosting account to set the MX records.

Google provides you with all of the information you need to make the changes to your existing MX records. Changing the records is mostly cutting and pasting the server names Google provides into the corresponding areas in your registrar's or website host's control panel for your account. It does require you to correctly navigate to the proper location in the control panel though to make the changes. See http://support.google.com/a/bin/answer.py?hl=en&answer=33352 for step-by-step directions if you are less familiar with this sort of activity.

Gmail Administrator's Control Panel

In addition to managing the entire Google Apps account, the Administrator's Control Panel has tools to manage the specific applications that are included, like Gmail. To access them, click the **Settings** tab at the top of the Administrator's Control Panel and then the **E-mail** tab on the left-hand side of the subsequent page.

Many of the e-mail settings are self explanatory, like **Name format** (last name first or first name first), **e-mail read receipts** (this sends you a message when someone opens your e-mail message), and **Offline Gmail** (which is described in Lesson 8). You probably want to enable **Offline Gmail**.

Many of the e-mail settings on the Administrator's Control Panel are hidden behind vague labels, so they are not so self-explanatory. We describe some of them in the following sections.

Controlling What Comes In and Goes Out Via E-mail

One potential source of security breaches is malicious attachments to e-mail messages. Clicking on any of these attachments can infect the recipient's computer (and, in some cases, the entire network) with malware, a virus, or worse. To limit this exposure, an Administrator can control the types of files that are allowed as attachments to inbound e-mails by creating **Attachment Compliance** filters (see Figure 19.2). Aside from inbound e-mails, these filters can also be applied to **Outbound** or **Internal** (**sending** or **receiving**) messages. In addition, exemptions from these filter rules can be made for one or more people.

Figure 19.2 E-mail Control Panel Filters

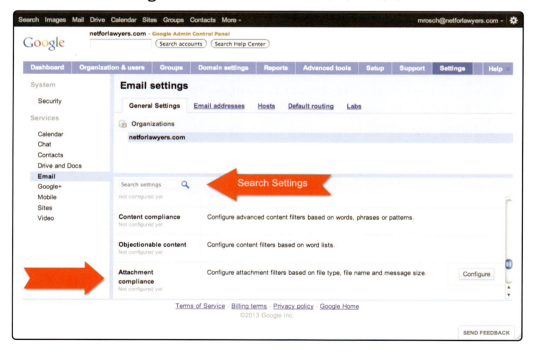

To limit these attachments, click **Settings** > **E-mail** > **General Settings** and then use the **Search Settings** box to search for *Attachment Compliance*. Once you've located the **Attachment Compliance** section, click the **Configure** button to the right of the title to create your filter (see Figure 19.2).

Click the **Add** button in the **Expressions** section of the pop-up window to select the types of attachments you do not want to allow. In the **Add expressions that describe the content you want to search for in each message** section, you can check the boxes next to the types of files you want to limit as attachments (see Figure 19.3). However, this list does not

Figure 19.3 E-mail Attachment Compliance

include some of the file types most likely to include malicious content, such as .rar or .reg files; you should add those yourself in the **Custom file types** box. Executable files (.exe) are automatically rejected by Gmail. In addition to **File type**, you can use the drop-down menu to limit **Message size** and **File name**.

In the section labeled **if the above expressions match, do the following** (not pictured in Figure 19.3), you can select how to **Modify** these messages: route the message to another recipient (usually the Administrator who wants to monitor this activity), **remove attachments from message** (which also adds a notice informing the recipient that the attachment was removed), or **Reject** the message (which also sends a notice to the sender informing them of the rejected status).

The **Options** section at the bottom of the **Attachment Compliance** pop-up window allows you to **Bypass this setting for messages to or from addresses or domains within these allowed lists** by listing e-mail addresses or entire domains that are exempt from these rules (not pictured in Figure 19.3).

> **PRACTICE TIP**
>
> Exemptions could be appropriate if attorneys needed to send photos, x-rays, or other image files to co-counsel or the opposition. Those attorneys' e-mail addresses or the domain name of the other firm could be exempt from these rules.

At the top of the pop-up window, you can **Add** [a] **description** of the setting that will appear in the **Settings** panel.

What to Do When an Employee Leaves the Firm

Just as you would ask an employee leaving the firm to return keys to the office, you should also take the keys to his or her e-mail account and any shared documents in the employee's Google Apps account.

Don't Delete the Account

The administrator can immediately cut off the employee's access to his or her account in a number of ways, including changing the password and suspending or deleting the account. Deleting the account is the most permanent. If you delete an account, you will not be able to retrieve that employee's client-related e-mail correspondence (or other information stored in that account) so a replacement employee can follow up on it—or for any other reason.

Changing a User's Password

The easiest method for terminating an employee's access to a company Google Apps account that still preserves the firm's access to the account is for the Administrator to change the password (see Figure 19.4).

To do this, click on the **Organizations & Users** tab in the Administrator's Control Panel and then click on the name of the user whose account you need to change. You'll then be prompted to enter (and confirm) a new password for this account. You can then give this new password to another employee to continue to access and monitor the account.

USAGE TIP

After changing the account password, you may also want to log into the account and set up a vacation responder to automatically reply to incoming e-mails, letting those senders know that the employee they're attempting to contact is no longer with the firm and giving them contact information for the employee(s) who will now be handling the departed employee's matters. The **Vacation responder** is on the **General** tab of the individual account's **Settings** menu.

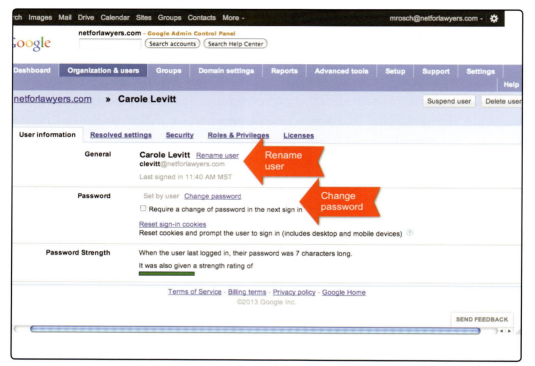

Figure 19.4 Change Password

When an employee's name changes (due to marriage, divorce, or some other reason) you can use the **Rename user** link next to the user's name in the **General** section to change the name on his or her account without losing any of the previous correspondence or documents.

> **USAGE TIP**
>
> You can also use the **Rename user** feature on this tab to reassign a former employee's account to a new employee who will be handling the departed employee's matters.

Suspending a User

In anticipation of litigation, it might become necessary to block a user's access to his or her account to prevent the employee from deleting or altering previous e-mails, documents, or calendar events. It is possible to **Suspend** the account (see Figure 19.4) by clicking the **Suspend** button in the upper right-hand corner of the screen where you change the account's password. Suspension basically locks the account from that point forward—no data can be added or deleted until the account is reinstated.

One downside to suspending an account is that incoming e-mails cannot be forwarded to another employee for a response. E-mails sent to the suspended address will just bounce back to the sender with a non-descriptive (**Delivery to the following recipient failed permanently**) message with no information on who the sender should contact. If you do need to "freeze" an account to preserve communication in it, suspension is the way to go.

Calendar's Administrator Control Panel

The Google Calendar Administrator Control Panel has only three tabs, as discussed below.

The Org Settings Tab

By default, users' primary Calendars are not shared outside of your firm. On the **Org Settings** tab, the Administrator can choose the highest level of internal and external sharing they will allow for the firm's users, from the most restrictive (sharing only free/busy information) to the least restrictive (sharing all information).

Individual users cannot change this setting, but from the allowed range they can set the sharing limits of individual events they add to their Calendars (e.g., **Default**, **Public**, **Private**).

The Org Settings tab is where you enable the **Labs** feature that allows users to install the experimental features discussed in Lesson 17.

The General Tab

Like the primary Calendars discussed in the previous section, by default each user's secondary Calendars are not shared outside of their firm.

External sharing options for secondary calendars can be set the same way as described earlier in this Lesson.

Individual users cannot change this setting, but they can set the sharing limits of individual events they add to their secondary calendars (e.g., **Default**, **Public**, **Private**).

The Resources Tab

In addition to adding events to your calendar, as described in Lesson 13, you can also add firm **Resources** (e.g., conference rooms, LCD projectors) that can be scheduled through the Calendar (see Figure 19.5a). Use the e-mail address displayed after you create your new resources to "invite" that resource (e.g., LCD projector) to an event (e.g., meeting) when you add it to your Calendar. Available Resources appear with a check mark next to them in the **Add: Rooms, etc.**, section of the event. Unavailable Resources appear with a circle with a slash through it next to them (see Figure 19.5b).

Lesson 19 Dashboard   **127**

Figures 19.5a–b Include Resources

Optional Extra Layer of Security

Google offers an optional extra layer of security that requires your users to enter a verification code (in addition to user name and password) when they sign into their account. The verification code is sent to the user's cell phone as a text or voice message. This two-step process reduces the probability of unauthorized access to the user's personal information and the firm's shared information. It is a good idea to enable this in your account and to enforce the use of both steps. Enabling 2-step authentication makes it more difficult for a hacker to gain unauthorized access to an account and all of the information it contains. Interestingly, it takes two steps in two separate areas of the Administrator's Control Panel to enable this feature in your account.

Allow Users to Turn On 2-step Authentication

The Administrator must complete to two tasks to turn on the **2-step Authentication**, and each user must complete one task. The first Administrator step is to click the **Advanced Tools** tab and scroll down to the **Authentication** section. Then check the box marked **Allow users to turn on 2-step authentication**.

It's important that after you complete this first task, you direct all of your users to https://accounts.google.com/SmsAuthConfig to configure the feature with their cell phone numbers *before* you move on to the second task. Anyone who has not completed this configuration before you move on to the Administrator's second task could be locked out of his or her account.

USAGE TIP

To confirm that all of your users have configured this feature, you can run a **2-Step Verification Enrollment Report** by clicking on the **Reports** tab and then the **Additional reports** sub-tab. Scroll down and click the **Download** button in the **2-Step Verification Enrollment Report** section to see who has or hasn't completed the 2-step verification process.

Turn On Enforcement of 2-Step Authentication

The second step the Administrator must take is to turn on enforcement of the 2-Step Authentication, which is done by clicking the **Settings** tab and then the **Security** tab on the left-hand side of the browser window. Then, in the **setting** window in the center portion of the browser window, scroll down and click the button to **Turn on enforcement** in the **2-step verification** section.

Lesson 20

Google Vault

While we've mostly looked at ways that law firms can use Gmail (and associated other tools in the Google Apps suite), one more recently introduced product, **Google Vault** (http://linkon.in/OOBwTV), is worth mentioning here, even though lawyers would be most interested in it for their clients' use.

Google Vault is an optional add-on service to Google Apps for Business accounts. It is useful for companies that must set retention policies for compliance audits or in anticipation of litigation. Google Vault allows companies to archive e-mail messages and chat sessions, as well as prepare to produce documents for e-discovery.

For an additional $5 per user per month, companies can:

- **Create retention policies.** Google Apps administrators have the power to define retention policies that are automatically applied to all users' e-mail and chat messages companywide, and to authorize access by other employees to do the same or to conduct investigations.

- **Archive e-mail and chat.** E-mail and chat messages are then automatically archived and retained according to those retention policies. Inadvertent (or intentional) deletions are avoided by the automated institution of the retention policies.

132 Google Gmail and Calendar in One Hour for Lawyers

- **Be prepared for E-discovery.** Google Vault includes powerful search tools to find and retrieve relevant e-mail and chat messages in the event they need to be produced for litigation or compliance audits.

- **Organize and create Matters.** In addition to being able to search for and retrieve relevant messages, Google Vault provides tools for the authorized investigator to create separate **Matters** to organize and manage the documents they find. This way, if a message is relevant to more than one matter, the investigator can include the same message in each matter that the message relates to.

- **Search to locate documents.** With powerful search limiters, investigators can create as broad or as narrow a search as necessary to retrieve the requested documents. Additionally, searches can be saved to re-run again in the future to retrieve updated results (or the same results, depending on the search criteria and retention policies).

- **Place holds on specific users' messages.** Google Apps administrators can place litigation holds on specific users as needed. When a user is placed on hold, he or she can't delete e-mail and chat messages.

- **Conduct audits.** Administrators can run reports on user activity through the archive after it's been created. Searches, message views, and exports, among other activities, can be tracked.

- **Export messages.** Specific e-mail and chat messages can be exported from the archive to an MBOX (standardized mailbox format) for additional processing and review by outside entities.

Lesson 21

Google Apps Marketplace and Chrome Web Store Plug-ins

In addition to all of the tools built into Google Apps and Gmail, Google and third-party developers are also creating separate tools that integrate with Gmail to further increase productivity. The **Google Apps Marketplace** is meant to be a "one-stop-shop" for tools to add functions to your Google Apps for Business account. Google's **Chrome Web Store** is a collection of plug-ins that work exclusively with the Chrome Web browser. Sometimes the same tools are found in both the web store and the Marketplace. Pricing varies by product. They range from free, to a few dollars per user per month. Most offer a free trial period.

Google Apps Marketplace

The tools in the **Google Apps Marketplace** (http://www.google.com/enterprise/marketplace/home) are all meant to be used with Google Apps. These tools can be added to your account with as little as a few clicks. Because the Google Apps suite "lives in the cloud," there's nothing to download to your computer to add these new tools. It's all done right in your browser. You can locate tools by keyword searching at the Marketplace.

After you keyword search the Google Apps Marketplace, you can use the chechboxes in the left-hand column to further refine your results by the type of apps you're looking for (e.g., **Mail Integration**, **Calendar Integration**) (see Figure 21.1).

Figure 21.1 Refine Marketplace Search

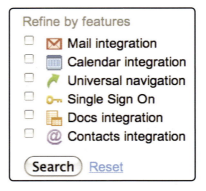

Google Chrome Web Store

The tools in the **Google Chrome Web Store** are all plug-ins meant to add functions to the Chrome Web browser. Not all of them are for use with Google Apps or Gmail. (A list of those plug-ins for Gmail is available at http://linkon.in/OZB8Tl.) Unlike the tools in the Marketplace, these require you to download and install the plug-in on your computer, which is not usually a difficult task.

Lesson 21 Google Apps Marketplace and Chrome Web Store Plug-ins **135**

Examples of Plug-ins Common to Marketplace and Web Store

In addition to Offline Gmail and Offline Calendar, discussed in Lessons 8 and 18 respectively, listed below are just a few of our other favorites from among the hundreds of tools that are available in the Marketplace and the Web Store:

Boomerang (http://linkon.in/OpFz8u). If you've ever wanted to write an e-mail right now while you were thinking about it—but didn't need to send it until tomorrow, or next week, then Boomerang is for you. Boomerang works as a plug-in to the Chrome and Firefox web browsers to allow you to schedule an e-mail to be sent at a later time and send you a reminder if you don't hear back from an e-mail recipient. Pricing ranges from free (to send 10 scheduled messages per month) to $14.99 per user per month (to send unlimited scheduled e-mails).

Rapportive (http://linkon.in/Ner76m). When you get an e-mail from someone, but you're not sure who they are or how you know them, Rapportive can come to the rescue. By aggregating the publicly available information from people's social networking profiles, this extension for the Chrome, Firefox, and Safari web browsers adds useful information into the e-mail's margin like a photo, job title, and links to the sender's Facebook, LinkedIn, and/or Twitter profiles all done by matching their e-mail address. Rapportive is free.

Lesson 22

Security, Confidentiality, and Ethics

Some of the first questions we get when discussing Google Apps are "What about the security and confidentiality of the information stored in those documents and e-mails? Is it secure enough for lawyers to use?" Although the answer to those questions depends on whom you ask, a growing numbers of attorneys and law firms have been answering "yes" and adopting Google Apps.

A number of critics question the security of any off-site web-based application or storage service, while others seem biased against only certain providers. Interest in the security of Google's cloud offerings has been renewed in light of the company's implementation of a new set of Terms of Service. Additionally, the widely reported move by the City of Los Angeles to halt implementation of Google Apps to its criminal justice entities, including the LAPD and the Criminal Division of the City Attorney's Office, has also raised security concerns. This is despite the fact that the Civil Division and other city agencies have completed the implementation of Google Apps.

On the other side of the coin, a growing number of state bar association ethics opinions approve of lawyers using these cloud services as long as the lawyers use reasonable measures to ensure the security of these services.

> **USAGE TIP**
>
> A common place where e-mail security is breached involves the user not logging out of their account on a shared/public computer (e.g., hotel business center). If you sign into Gmail from multiple computers, but are worried you may have forgotten to sign out of one, you can sign out remotely. At the bottom of your **Inbox**, you'll see information about the time and location of the last activity on your account. Click **Details** to see whether your account is still open in another location and click the **Sign out all other sessions** button to close all other open sessions. Also, see the **Usage Tip**, *Using a Public Computer like Those in a Hotel's Business Center is Not Recommended* (page xxii in the Introduction), warning against using public computers.

To get a better handle on Google's security measures, we spoke with Marc S. Crandall, JD, CIPP, Google's Head of Global Compliance, Enterprise. He addresses compliance issues concerning the development and deployment of Google technology. Crandall has also served as Product Counsel for a number of services, including Gmail (where he focused on laws and regulations dealing with privacy, system security, intellectual property, content regulation, telecommunications, and consumer protections). He was also involved in the successful review of Google Apps for Business to determine whether it met Federal Information Security Management Act of 2000 (FISMA) standards, 44 U.S.C. § 3541, et seq. (FISMA requires each covered federal agency to develop and implement security practices for its electronic information that comply with standards published by the National Institute for Standards and Technology (NIST). Google Apps was certified as being FISMA-compliant by the U.S. General Services Agency in 2010.)

Beyond the FISMA certification, Google has also successfully completed two more independently verified (Statement on Standards for Attestation Engagements) SSAE 16 Type II audit and (International Standards Organization) ISO 27001 certification.

> **PRACTICE TIP**
>
> "As a law firm handling confidential information for our clients, Bradford & Barthel takes security extremely seriously," said the firm's Director of Knowledge Strategy and Technology, Eric Hunter in a in a guest post on the Official Google Enterprise Blog (http://linkon.in/VvM3pL). "We're responsible for private information on individuals and companies, and our best security option is Google Apps," he continued. "Google has many security features—SAS70 [now SSAE 16] Type II certification and two-step verification included—that allow us to feel confident our data and the data of our clients is much safer than if we hosted it on premise."

SSAE 16 (formerly SAS70; http://www.ssae16.org/what-is-ssae-16/ssae-16-definition.html) is a set of standards developed by the Auditing Standards Board (ASB) of the American Institute of Certified Public Accountants (AICPA) meant to determine, in part, whether companies were living up to claims made about the services they provide. Originally developed for financial services companies and their service providers, the audits have more recently been utilized by other types of service providers—particularly cloud-computing and data-hosting companies. An independent Certified Public Accountant conducts the audit to determine if a company is SSAE 16 Type II-compliant. The Grant Thornton accounting firm conducted the Google Apps SSAE 16 Type II audit.

ISO 27001 (http://www.27000.org/iso-27001.htm) is a set of information security management system standards designed to "provide a model for establishing, implementing, operating, monitoring, reviewing, maintaining, and improving an Information Security Management System." An independent external auditor performs the final Certification Audit to determine whether ISO 27001 compliance has been met. A division of the Ernst & Young accounting firm conducted the Google Apps ISO 27001 audit.

> **PRACTICE TIP**
>
> "While FISMA provides some comfort, I think that other security certifications (SSAE 16 Type II audits and ISO 27001) that Google reports it has obtained are more meaningful for attorneys," says David G. Ries, Partner at Thorp Reed & Armstrong, LLP and co-author of *Locked Down: Information Security for Lawyers* (ABA LPM 2012). Ries explains that, "SSAE 16 Type II audits and ISO 27001 certification are security requirements that technology attorneys regularly advise clients to try to get into contracts with service providers (including data centers and cloud services) that will have access to their confidential data. These certifications have substantially reduced my personal concerns about Gmail and Google Apps. While I use them personally, I plan to do some more due diligence before using them for confidential client information. What I have seen so far looks good."

Google also participates in the Safe Harbor Program of the European Union (EU) and the United States (http://export.gov/safeHarbor/), which identifies U.S. companies that have implemented security and privacy standards stringent enough to meet EU requirements for the storage of that information. This program allows companies in the EU to transfer data to U.S. companies that certify their compliance with the standards of the Safe Harbor Program. Companies self-certify their compliance with the program's requirements.

> **USAGE TIP**
>
> Even with the security measures Google has in place for Google Apps, you still have a responsibility to make your account as secure as possible by at least using a strong (hard-to-guess) password and 2-step authentication to access your account. (See Lesson 19 for more details about 2-step authentication.) You should also continually focus on security in everyday use of any technology.
>
> Like many technology companies, Google has continued to add security enhancements to Google Apps over time. For example, in 2007, Google acquired Postini, a well-regarded e-mail and web security and archiving service provider. Google originally offered its service by subscription to larger customers, but has been recently integrating them into Google Apps. As this book went to press, Google announced plans to integrate Message Security into Google Apps for Business and is working on integrating Message Encryption (http://postini-transition.googleapps.com). In 2010, Google announced the availability of 2-step authentication as an optional security measure. Attorneys should monitor the availability of these kinds of added security features and adopt them where appropriate. The seamless addition of these kinds of upgraded security features is one of the benefits of using cloud apps.

Your Information in Your Google Apps Account Is Backed Up in Multiple Locations and Multiple Computers

"A primary benefit of moving to the cloud is to leverage Google's resources to enhance the confidentiality, integrity, and availability of a user's data—the critical elements of sound information security practices. Users benefit from the same formidable infrastructure that Google uses to support its own operations," says Crandall. "Any single user's computer can crash or otherwise become unavailable. Google Apps offers geographic redundancy, so that the data is backed up in multiple locations and multiple computers, helping ensure access to that data should any one computer become unavailable. Users also benefit from the collective expertise of Google's information security personnel."

You *Do* Own Your Information in Google Apps and Gmail

Some critics of lawyers' use of Google Apps point to the company-wide *consumer* Google Terms of Service (TOS; http://www.google.com/intl/en/policies/terms/) as evidence that Google controls the information you store in these accounts. Specifically, many critics point to the provisions in the "Your Content in Our Services" section that grants Google a "worldwide license to . . . publish, publicly perform, publicly display and distribute" any of the information in the Docs you store online. (Similar language was also included in Paragraph 11.1 of the previous [April 16, 2007] version of the TOS at http://www.google.com/intl/en/policies/terms/archive/20070416/.) Critics claim that this essentially gives Google ownership over the information stored in Google Docs or Gmail.

"Those [critics'] concerns are misguided," says Google's Crandall. "First, these critics are referring to the wrong terms of service. They are referencing the terms that cover many of Google's *consumer* [emphasis added] services. These services include everything from Blogger to Google Reader. As Google Apps is an enterprise service, Google utilizes a different set of terms that specifically address business-oriented concerns. In fact, this agreement [the Google Apps for Business Online Agreement (see below)] addresses the sensitivity of enterprise users' confidential information."

Second, Crandall notes that, "the language of the 'Your Content in Our Services' section of the consumer Terms of Service is included because under copyright law, Google requires a license from users to display or transmit the users' content. So to show a blog, we ask the user to provide Google with a license to the blog's content—the same applies for any other service where users can create content. But in all these cases, the license is limited to providing the service," says Crandall. "What belongs to you stays yours."

In its Google Apps for Business Online Agreement, Google goes to great lengths to explain that users do own the information they store within Google's services. Unfortunately, Google does not make this information easy to locate. The Google Apps for Business Online Agreement, which Crandall mentions, governs information stored in Apps for Business accounts and can be found at http://www.google.com/apps/intl/en/terms/premier_terms.html.

Section 6 of the Agreement is plainly labeled "Confidential Information." Paragraph 6.1 ("Obligations") states in part that, "Each party will: (a) protect the other party's Confidential Information with the same standard of care it uses to protect its own Confidential Information." Paragraph 6.2 covers the limited "Exceptions" to the confidentiality obligations (e.g., information "the recipient of the Confidential Information already knew). Paragraph 6.3 ("Required Disclosure") lists instances in which, "Each party may disclose the other party's Confidential Information when required by law but only after it, if legally permissible: (a) uses commercially reasonable efforts to notify the other party; and (b) gives the other party the chance to challenge the disclosure." With the inclusion of this language in the Google Apps-specific agreement, it seems reasonable to conclude that Google does *not* claim ownership of your e-mail or documents stored at Google and that your documents and e-mail remain confidential.

Paragraph 7.1 of that same Agreement (Intellectual Property Rights) clearly states, "Except as expressly set forth herein, this Agreement does not grant either party any rights, implied or otherwise, to the other's content or any of the other's intellectual property. As between the parties, Customer owns all Intellectual Property Rights in Customer Data, and Google owns all Intellectual Property Rights in the Services." Here Google is reserving its intellectual property rights in the Google Apps technology—not the material saved in your Google Apps accounts.

Even the free version of Google's Apps, for those who still have access to these types of accounts, carries similar provisions. (The Agreement/Terms of Service for free Google Apps accounts can be found at http://www.google.com/apps/intl/en/terms/standard_terms.html.) "Finally, the Google Privacy Policy [http://www.google.com/apps/intl/en/terms/user_terms.html] specifically describes under what circumstances user information can be shared with third parties," points out Crandall. He also notes that while there were recent widely reported changes to the Privacy Policy, the Terms of Service specific to Google Apps always applies.

Seventeen Thousand City of Los Angeles Employees Use Google Apps

In the fall of 2011, it was widely reported that the City of Los Angeles was halting the deployment of Google Apps for Government to its police department, renewing criticism of the security measures Google provides to the customers of its cloud-based services. This halt was not generated by the city itself. It was based on a set of standards for data storage and security developed by the nation's law enforcement community for specific types of criminal justice-related information.

Administered by the FBI's Criminal Justice Information Services Division (CJIS) the policy includes: "prohibiting the performance of remote maintenance from locations outside the United States," and "requiring fingerprint-based background checks on their system/database/security/network administrators who have the capability to access and recompile criminal justice information." In interviews, the city's Chief Technology officer Randi Levin went on record as saying, "Google Apps is 'working fine' for the majority of city employees" (http://linkon.in/ICqizC).

"We're disappointed that the city introduced requirements for the LAPD after the contract was signed that are, in its own words, 'currently incompatible with cloud computing,'" Andrew Kovacs, a Google spokesperson said in a statement at the time. He added that, "we are meeting our commitments to the City of Los Angeles. Indeed, the City recently renewed its Google Apps contract for 17,000 employees [outside of the areas dealing with these criminal records], and the project is expected to save Los Angeles taxpayers millions of dollars. The City has acknowledged Google Apps is more secure than its current system. Along the way they've also introduced new requirements which require work [by any vendor] to implement in a cloud computing environment, and we've presented a plan to meet them at no additional cost." (http://linkon.in/Hqu0uo)

In a separate statement, the FBI stressed that its CJIS requirements were "cloud-compatible," albeit, "tough for some vendors to meet." (http://linkon.in/HyEau3)

How many law firms require fingerprinting of their own IT staff (or of outsourced IT consultants)? Furthermore, it's important to note that CJIS-like standards, or for that matter, standards that apply to the handling of classified information, do not apply to the kinds of client-confidential data stored by law firms.

Are Google Apps Secure Enough for Lawyers to Meet Their "Confidentiality" Ethical Obligations?

Google's Crandall makes a strong case for the security of Google Apps for Business when he says, "Google trusts it for its own data, intellectual property, and trade secrets. Whether it is secure enough to meet ethical requirements is a question for the Bars. As with any outsourced service however, the question really is 'does the benefit outweigh the perceived risk?'"

As we dug deeper into the question of how Google vets its data center employees and controls those employees' access to customer-stored data, a Google corporate spokesperson referred us to Google's 2011 Security Whitepaper: Google Apps Messaging and Collaboration Products (http://linkon.in/WDZTK4). This document explains that beyond the usual employment, education, and reference checks, Google may also conduct criminal, credit, immigration, and security checks where local labor law or statutory regulations permit. Furthermore, "Upon acceptance of employment at Google, all employees are required to execute a confidentiality agreement and . . . the confidentiality and privacy of customer information and data is emphasized in the [employee] handbook and during new employee orientation. . . . In addition, each Google employee is required to read, understand, and take a training course on the company's Code of Conduct.

The code outlines Google's expectation that every employee will conduct business lawfully, ethically, with integrity, and with respect for each other and the company's users, partners, and even competitors. The Google Code of Conduct is available to the public at http://investor. google.com/corporate/code-of-conduct.html.

The whitepaper goes on to explain that, "Access rights and levels are based on [the Google] employee's job function and role, using the concepts of least-privilege and need-to-know to match access privileges to defined responsibilities. Google employees are only granted a limited set of default permissions to access company resources . . . requests for additional access follow a formal process that involves a request and an approval from a data or system owner, manager, or other executives, as dictated by Google's security policies." All access and permissions are tied to the employee's company-issued User ID. Because of these processes, most senior executives at Google do not have access to these portions of the networks—regardless of their titles. Note that this document also addresses Network and Operating System security measures implemented by Google.

(Also see the security measures listed in **The Health and Security of the Servers That House Your Data Are Monitored 24/7** section, on page xxiv of the Introduction.)

The ABA Commission on Ethics 20/20

The ABA Commission on Ethics 20/20 (http://linkon.in/kXGjmL) grappled with the question of whether and how lawyers might deal with "confidentiality issues arising from technology." The Commission made a recommendation to the ABA House of Delegates "designed to give lawyers more guidance regarding their confidentiality-related obligations when using technology," (http://linkon.in/k2UrLS).

At the 2012 ABA Annual Meeting, the House of Delegates approved the suggested revisions to Model Rule 1.6 (http://linkon.in/OYJIlc) to add a Paragraph (c) to read "A lawyer shall make reasonable efforts to prevent the inadvertent disclosure of, or unauthorized access to, information relating to the representation of a client." Also approved was the amendment of Comment 16 to that Rule (now renumbered as Comment 18) which reads in part, "Factors to be considered in determining the reasonableness of the lawyer's efforts include, but are not limited to, the sensitivity of the information, the likelihood of disclosure if additional safeguards are not employed, the cost of employing additional safeguards, [and] the difficulty of implementing the safeguards . . ." (http://linkon.in/SlKH3u).

Cloud services like Google Apps make "additional safeguards" (like highly-trained security engineers, third-party audited security practices, and redundant backups) available to every user.

But what would be the standard of "reasonable efforts" in these matters? State Bar Associations have been grappling with this ethics questions as far back as 2005 and while all of the ethics opinions published to date have concluded that it is permissible for lawyers to use these kinds of remote electronic storage services, they have arrived at their conclusions using varied arguments. The following is a summary of many of the state bar ethics opinions about cloud computing. They are listed from the earliest opinion to the latest. Additionally, we have created an online resource that includes analysis of these and other related ethics opinions at http://linkon.in/ethicsofcloud. New opinions will be added to the online list as they are published.

The State Bar of Arizona's Ethics Opinion 05-04 (2005)

For example, in 2005 the State Bar of Arizona's Ethics Opinion 05-04: Electronic Storage; Confidentiality (http://linkon.in/jAmXSI), the Bar concluded that electronic storage of client files is permissible as long as lawyers and law firms "take competent and reasonable steps to assure that the client's confidences are not disclosed to third parties through theft or inadvertence. In addition, an attorney or law firm is obligated to take reasonable and competent steps to assure that the client's electronic information is not lost or destroyed. In order to do that, an attorney must be competent to evaluate the nature of the potential threat to client electronic files and to evaluate and deploy appropriate computer hardware and software to accomplish that end. An attorney who lacks or cannot reasonably obtain that competence is ethically required to retain an expert consultant who does have such competence."

Google's Crandall suggests that "lawyers have to ask themselves if they're doing their clients a disservice by *not* storing their e-mail in the cloud. They have to ask themselves if they or their in-house IT team have a greater ability to keep their data secure than the engineering team at Google."

The New Jersey Advisory Committee on Professional Ethics Opinion 701 (2006)

In 2006, the New Jersey Advisory Committee on Professional Ethics addressed the question of "Electronic Storage and Access of Client Files" in Opinion 701–4/24/06 (http://linkon.in/V9nT82). In that Opinion, the New Jersey Committee stated, "The critical requirement under RPC 1.6, therefore, is that the attorney 'exercise reasonable care' against the possibility of unauthorized access to client information. A lawyer is required to exercise sound professional judgment on the steps necessary to secure client confidences against foreseeable attempts at unauthorized access. 'Reasonable care,' however, does not mean that the lawyer absolutely and strictly guarantees that the information will be utterly invulnerable against all unauthorized access. Such a guarantee is impossible, and a lawyer can no more guarantee against unauthorized access to electronic information than he can guarantee that a burglar will not break into his file room, or that someone will not illegally intercept his mail or steal a fax."

The Maine State Bar Professional Ethics Commission Opinion 194 (2008)

In 2008, the Maine State Bar Professional Ethics Commission addressed the question of "Client Confidences: Confidential firm data held electronically and handled by technicians for third-party vendors." In its Opinion 194–6/30/08 (http://linkon.in/lDtH2q), the Maine Commission concluded that, "with appropriate safeguards, an attorney may utilize transcription and computer server backup services remote from both the lawyer's physical office and the lawyer's direct control or supervision without violating the attorney's ethical obligation to maintain client confidentiality."

Along those same lines, Crandall observed that "there's a certain degree of trust involved when working with any third-party entity." Making an analogy to a vendor relationship most people would be familiar with, Crandall suggested, "let's look at banks. Most of us keep money in banks and not under a mattress. We have to trust that there are systems in place that keep bank employees from accessing our money. Even at a firm with an in-house IT team, there can be 15 people with root access to the network. Further, Google's model of providing customers with granular access of who has access to data stored in the cloud—the fundamental means of how Google docs are accessed—may be viewed as a significant upgrade to the 'reasonable care' standard that lawyers are held to for confidentiality. There's an argument that can be made that storing privileged documents on USB sticks, CDs, and elsewhere at some point won't be considered 'reasonable care' unless the documents are access-controlled in some way—as is the default with our cloud product."

The New York State Bar Association's Committee on Professional Ethics 820 (2008)

Also in 2008, the New York State Bar Association's Committee on Professional Ethics Opinion 820–2/8/08 (http://linkon.in/b7xZE1) concluded that "A lawyer may use an e-mail service provider that conducts computer scans of e-mails to generate computer advertising, where the e-mails are not reviewed by or provided to other individuals." While not named in the Opinion, the question's description of an "e-mail service provider that scans e-mails for advertising purposes" clearly describes Gmail.

The State Bar of Arizona Ethics Opinion 09-04 (2009)

In 2009, the State Bar of Arizona addressed a question similar to the one addressed by Maine the previous year. In Ethics Opinion 09-04: Confidentiality; Maintaining Client Files; Electronic Storage; Internet (http://linkon.in/iWybej), Arizona cited back to its 2005 Opinion and New Jersey's 2006 Opinion to validate attorneys' use of remote electronic file storage systems, and stated that the "lawyer's duty to take reasonable precautions does not require a guarantee that the system will be invulnerable to unauthorized access." The Bar went on to state that "the Committee also recognizes that technology advances may make certain protective measures obsolete over time. Therefore, the Committee does not suggest that the protective measures at issue in Ethics Op. 05-04 or in this Opinion necessarily satisfy ER 1.6's requirements indefinitely. Instead, whether a particular system provides reasonable protective measures must be 'informed by the technology reasonably available at the time to secure data against unintentional disclosure.' N.J. Ethics Op. 701. As technology advances occur, lawyers should periodically review security measures in place to ensure that they still reasonably protect the security and confidentiality of the clients' documents and information."

The New York State Bar Association's Committee on Professional Ethics Opinion 842 (2010)

In 2010, the New York State Bar Association's Committee on Professional Ethics Opinion 842–9/10/10 (http://linkon.in/jWYtJq) used language similar to Arizona Opinion 09-04 to allow lawyers to use cloud storage systems. In a similar vein, Google's Crandall poses the hypothetical, "Is the firm's in-house IT team keeping up with and installing every security patch? Are they patching every machine?" Google has teams of engineers dedicated to information security. Google also offers the added security of 2-step verification to all versions of Google Apps. This added layer of security requires you to enter a verification code in addition to your username and password, in order to sign into your Google Apps account from a device for the first time (see page 128). These verification codes can be generated using a smartphone app (on Android, Blackberry,

Google Gmail and Calendar in One Hour for Lawyers

or iOS devices) or may be sent via text message or phone call to your smartphone, cellphone, or landline phone.

The State Bar of California Standing Committee on Professional Responsibility and Conduct: Formal Opinion 2010-179 (2010)

The State Bar of California Standing Comittee on Prefessional Responsibity's (COPRAC's). Opinion 2010-179 (http://linkon.in/Y4gA2c) does not use the term "cloud computing," but the opinion can still be used to guide attorneys on their use of cloud computing because it deals with "using technology to transmit or store confidential client information when the technology may be susceptible to unauthorized access by third parties." The 2010-179 opinion explains that, "An attorney's duties of confidentiality and competence require the attorney to take appropriate steps to ensure that his or her use of technology in conjunction with a client's representation does not subject confidential client information to an undue risk of unauthorized disclosure. Because of the evolving nature of technology and differences in security features that are available, the attorney must ensure the steps are sufficient for each form of technology being used and must continue to monitor the efficacy of such steps."

The opinion explains that if client information is highly sensitive and a particular technology presents a risk of disclosure, then the attorney needs to consider other alternatives unless the client provides informed consent. (See also page 157 for a related California opinion.)

The Oregon State Bar Association's Formal Ethics Opinion 2011-188 (2011)

In the Oregon State Bar Association's Formal Ethics Opinion Number 2011-188 (http://linkon.in/vyiETi), the Bar offered a "Yes, qualified" answer to the question of whether lawyers may contract "with third-party vendor[s] to store client files and documents online on [a] remote server so that Lawyer and/or Client could access the documents over the Internet from any remote location." In offering this guidance, the Opinion points to Oregon RPC 1.6, which covers the attorney's duty to "not reveal information relating to the representation of a client."

The Oregon Opinion stated, in part, that "[a] Lawyer may store client materials on a third-party server so long as Lawyer complies with the duties of competence and confidentiality to reasonably keep the client's information secure within a given situation. To do so, the lawyer must take reasonable steps to ensure that the storage company will reliably secure client data and keep information confidential. Under certain circumstances, this may be satisfied though a third-party vendor's compliance with industry standards relating to confidentiality and security, provided that those industry standards meet the minimum requirements imposed on the Lawyer by the Oregon RPCs."

The Iowa State Bar Ethics Opinion 11-01 (2011)

The Iowa State Bar Ethics Opinion 11-01 (http://linkon.in/uQd9YQ) pointed to Comment 17 to Iowa's Rule 32:1.6 (http://linkon.in/HQgjcK) as establishing a "reasonable and flexible approach to guide a lawyer's use of ever-changing technology. It recognizes that the degree of protection to be afforded client information varies with the client, matter, and information involved. But it places on the lawyer the obligation to perform due diligence to assess the degree of protection that will be needed and to act accordingly." Also, recognizing the changing nature of cloud computing services, the Iowa Opinion chose to offer "basic guidance regarding the implementation of the standard described in Comment 17," in the form of a list of considerations lawyers should take into account when performing their due diligence in reviewing cloud services for their firms.

The North Carolina Bar Association 2011 Formal Ethics Opinion 6 (2011)

The North Carolina Bar Association's 2011 Formal Ethics Opinion 6 (http://linkon.in/Q2Lpx5), like New York Opinion #842, answers two separate questions regarding lawyers' subscribing to software as a service (SaaS) rather than purchasing and installing software from disks. First, the North Carolina Opinion tackles whether lawyers should even be using SaaS products at all "for case or practice management, document management, and billing/financial management," or "the storage of a law firm's data, including client files, billing information, and work product, on remote servers rather than on the law firm's own computer and, therefore, outside the direct control of the firm's lawyers." The Opinion answered this question by stating, "Yes, provided steps are taken to minimize the risk of inadvertent or unauthorized disclosure of confidential client information and to protect client property, including the information in a client's file, from risk of loss." The Opinion points to Comments 17 and 18 of North Carolina's Rule of Professional Conduct 1.6: "Comment [17] explains, 'A lawyer must act competently to safeguard information relating to the representation of a client against inadvertent or unauthorized disclosure by the lawyer or other persons who are participating in the representation of the client or who are subject to the lawyer's supervision.' Comment [18] adds that, when transmitting confidential client information, a lawyer must take 'reasonable precautions to prevent the information from coming into the hands of unintended recipients.'"

In addition the Opinion tackles what measures lawyers should take to assess SaaS vendors to minimize potential security risks. Recognizing that criteria for assessing the security of these SaaS services would change with technology, the Opinion outlines a list of points lawyers should consider, rather than spelling out a specific set of guidelines lawyers must follow. The Opinion introduces this list with the following caveat: "This opinion does not set forth specific security requirements because mandatory security measures would create a false sense of security in an environment where the risks are continually changing. Instead, due diligence and frequent and regular education are required." Some of the security measures the Opinions suggest be considered are:

- a specific agreement covering "how the vendor will handle confidential client information in keeping with the lawyer's professional responsibilities"
- the ability to retrieve the lawyer's data if "the SaaS vendor goes out of business, or the service otherwise has a break in continuity"
- careful review of the SaaS license agreement and security policy
- evaluation of security measures, "including, but not limited to, firewalls, encryption techniques, socket security features, and intrusion-detection systems"
- evaluation of the SaaS vendors' backup policies for the lawyer's data

The Pennsylvania Bar Association Formal Opinion 2011-200 (2011)

In its Formal Opinion 2011-200, the Pennsylvania Bar Association's Committee on Legal Ethics and Professional Responsibility specifically addressed the question, "May an attorney ethically store confidential client material in 'the cloud'?" The committee's conclusion is a qualified "yes."

Like some of the other opinions on this topic, Pennsylvania Opinion 2011-200 instructs attorneys that they "may ethically allow client confidential material to be stored in 'the cloud' provided the attorney takes reasonable care to assure that (1) all such materials remain confidential, and (2) reasonable safeguards are employed to ensure that the data is [sic] protected from breaches, data loss, and other risks."

Like North Carolina Opinion 6, discussed in the previous section, this opinion includes a bullet point list describing what "the standard of reasonable care for 'cloud computing' may include."

In addition to addressing the whole category of cloud computing services that lawyers might use, the Pennsylvania opinion also points to the use of web-based e-mail (naming Gmail among others) as "ordinarily permissible" for lawyers in most circumstances but, "may not be acceptable in the context of a particularly heightened degree of concern or in a particular set of facts."

The Massachusetts Bar Association Ethics Opinion 12-03 (2012)

Massachusetts Bar Association Ethics Opinion 12-03 (http://linkon. in/Mgqw4j) specifically addressed the question of "whether it [the use of cloud computing] would violate Lawyer's obligations under the Massachusetts Rules of Professional Conduct to store confidential client information using 'Google docs' or some other Internet-based storage solution, and to synchronize his computers and other devices that contain or access such information over the Internet."

In finding the use of cloud services permissible, the Massachusetts Opinion analogizes cloud services to "lawyer's use of unencrypted Internet e-mail to engage in confidential communications with his or her client" and third-party vendors accessing law firm networks in order to maintain the firm's hardware or software, which the Bar had found permissible in previous Opinions.

Like the other Opinions previously discussed in this Lesson, Massachusetts instructs lawyers to undertake "reasonable efforts to ensure that the provider's terms of use and data-privacy policies, practices, and procedures are compatible with the lawyer's professional obligations, including the obligation to protect confidential client information reflected in Rule 1.6(a)." Unlike some other Opinions discussed here, the Massachusetts Opinion states that lawyers should get their clients' prior consent before, "storing or transmitting particularly sensitive client information by means of the Internet."

The State Bar of California Standing Committee on Professional Responsibility and Conduct: Formal Opinion 2012-184 (2012)

In 2012 Opinion 2012-184 (http://linkon.in/UXr4Qw), the State Bar of California's COPRAC took its second look at technology and client confidentiality. Unlike its earlier opinion (Opinion 2010-179; see page 152) this time they actually used the term "cloud computing." However, they added a new twist by focusing on a virtual law office practice ("VLO") and asked whether an attorney can "maintain a virtual law office practice ('VLO') and still comply with her ethical obligations if the communications with the client, and storage of and access to all information about the client's matter, are all conducted solely through the Internet using the secure computer servers of a third-party vendor (i.e., 'cloud computing')"

The opinion explained that "As it pertains to the use of technology, the Business and Professions Code and the Rules of Professional Conduct do not impose greater or different duties upon a VLO practitioner operating in the cloud than they do upon an attorney practicing in a traditional law office. While an attorney may maintain a VLO in the cloud where communications with the client, and storage of and access to all information about the client's matter, are conducted solely via the Internet using a third-party's secure servers, Attorney may be required to take additional steps to confirm that she is fulfilling her ethical obligations due to distinct issues raised by the hypothetical VLO and its operation. Failure of Attorney to comply with all ethical obligations relevant to these issues will preclude the operation of a VLO in the cloud as described herein." The opinion refers attorneys back to Opinion 2010-179 for a fuller discussion on the analysis that the Committee believes attorneys should undertake when considering the use of a particular form of technology. (See the quote on page 152 from Opinion 2010-179 for a synopsis of the analysis attorneys should undertake.)

The Florida Bar Standing Professional Ethics Committee: Proposed Advisory Opinion 12-3 (2013)

In its January 2013 Proposed Advisory Opinion 12-3, addressing the question of whether lawyers can use cloud computing resources in their practices (http://linkon.in/Y5jgtb), The Florida Bar's Professional Ethics Committee concludes that, "lawyers may use cloud computing if they take reasonable precautions to ensure that confidentiality of client information is maintained. The lawyer should research the service provider to be used, should ensure that the service provider maintains adequate security, should ensure that the lawyer has adequate access to the information stored remotely, and should consider backing up the data elsewhere as a precaution." This opinion specifically cites a number of the Opinions already discussed here, when stating, "This Committee agrees with the opinions issued by the states that have addressed the issue. Cloud computing is permissible as long as the lawyer adequately addresses the potential risks associated with it. As indicated by other states that have addressed the issue, lawyers must perform due diligence in researching the outside service provider(s) to ensure that adequate safeguards exist to protect information stored by the service provider(s)." The Florida Bar's Proposed Advisory Opinion 12-3 also refers to New York State Bar Ethics Opinion 842 and Iowa Ethics Opinion 11-01 (both discussed earlier in this Lesson) for guidance on due diligence steps lawyers should take when considering a particular cloud computing provider.

No Differences in Security Between Free and Paid Google Products

Because Google offers various versions of Google Apps, other questions arise about the relative security of the free version of Google Apps versus the Business and the Government offerings. (While you can no longer open a new, free Google Apps account, any company that opened one prior to December 2012 can still retain those free accounts.) Conventional wisdom would lead us to believe that the free version of Google Apps would have fewer security safeguards in place than the paid versions. Crandall explains that this is not the case.

"The security measures in place to protect the paid Business accounts are similar to those in place for the free version of Google Apps," he stressed. "There are a lot of ways Google can add value for the Business and Government customers that don't involve less security for the free customer. Some of those added features include the SLA [Service Level Agreement] guarantee [the promise of uptime availability of the Google Apps], access to dedicated phone support, migration services, whether advertising is displayed to users, etc. All versions provide administrators with the ability to force the use of SSL [the Secure Sockets Layer encrypted connection], set password length requirements, and view password strength indicators. Offering less security [to a customer using the free version of Google Apps] doesn't make any sense."

In March 2011, Microsoft accused Google of inflating claims that its Apps for Government offering had received FISMA certification, when it was the Business offering that had received the certification. Google countered that the Government accounts were a subset of Business accounts. The U.S. General Service Administration agreed with Google's assertion. In fact, the General Services Administration is now using Google Apps for Government.

In our interview, Crandall reiterated, "the Government service is a subset of the Business service. Apps for Government is still a multi-tenant hosting environment, but only government data are stored on those machines. The servers are also physically segregated from the non-government servers, in separate locked cages. The servers are all located domestically, but the security measures are similar."

Conclusion

We think that the conclusion of the Massachusetts Bar Association's recent Ethics Opinion 12-03, permitting lawyers' use of cloud computing, sites sums up the dilemma nicely, "The Committee further observes that Google docs and other Internet based storage solutions, like many, if not most, remotely accessible software systems and computer networks, are not immune from attack by unauthorized persons or other forms of security breaches." The Opinion went on to state, "Ultimately, the question of whether the use of Google docs, or any other Internet-based data storage service provider, is compatible with Lawyer's ethical obligation to protect his clients' confidential information is one that Lawyer must answer for himself based on the criteria set forth in this opinion, the information that he is reasonably able to obtain regarding the relative security of the various alternatives that are available, and his own sound professional judgment."

While no file storage option is foolproof or hacker proof, cloud computing and storage services like Google Apps can give law firms of all sizes the benefit of an engineering team (probably better-trained than the firm could afford to hire on its own) to manage the security and availability of their data.

We agree with the Massachusetts Opinion's conclusion that it's up to individual attorneys to decide if they are comfortable trusting their clients' documents to the cloud.

For example, an attorney involved in an M&A deal might decide that the benefits of using a cloud service like Google Apps do not outweigh the risk of a hacker gaining access to confidential information in a multi-million dollar deal. On the other hand, an estate planning attorney working on a small estate or a family attorney making a minor change to a custody agreement might decide the benefits of using the cloud outweigh the risk.

Lesson 22 Security, Confidentiality, and Ethics **161**

> ### PRACTICE TIP
>
> ## Beyond Ethical Considerations: Common Law Duties to Safeguard Client Information
>
> In addition to these ethical duties, David G. Ries, Partner at Thorp Reed & Armstrong, LLP explains that "attorneys have common law duties to safeguard information relating to clients. Common law duties generally parallel the ethics requirements, requiring reasonable measures, and breach can result in a malpractice or professional negligence action. Attorneys may also have contractual and regulatory duties to protect information about clients and others. Some clients, particularly those in regulated industries, impose contractual security obligations on their attorneys. Federal and state laws and regulations may also require protection of specified information about individuals, like Social Security numbers and financial and health information." For more information on this topic, see "Safeguarding Confidential Data: Your Ethical and Legal Obligations," by David G. Ries, *Law Practice, Volume 36, Number 4, page 49 (July/August 2010)*, http://linkon.in/SDqdyk.

Appendix A

What Is Cloud Computing?*

Although you may think that you are unfamiliar with cloud computing, rest assured that you have already used it in one form or another. If you have ever used Gmail, Hotmail, or Yahoo! mail as your e-mail platform, or if you have exchanged e-mails with someone who uses one of these e-mail platforms, then your e-mails have been stored in the cloud. If you are a member of Facebook or LinkedIn, then you use an Internet service based in the cloud. If you store and share your photos online using Flickr, Picasa, Shutterfly, or Snapfish, then you use cloud computing. If you have ever obtained information from Wikipedia, you have accessed an encyclopedia based entirely in the cloud. When you listen to music using Pandora, watch a television show on Hulu, view YouTube videos, or stream a movie from Netflix, you are consuming media stored in the cloud. Cloud computing is undoubtedly part of your day-to-day life, whether you realize it or not.

"Most attorneys already use a minor form of cloud computing, e-mail. They may not know it, but their e-mail service is generally outsourced to an ISP. Expanding to other cloud-computing services is a natural extension of the trust they put with their e-mail provider," says Jonathan Jaffe of Jonathan Jaffe Law, Oakland, California.

---

* Excerpted from *Cloud Computing for Lawyers* 1-3, by Nicole Black, American Bar Association (2012)

Cloud computing gets its name from the flowcharts used to diagram networked computing. In this context, a cloud is used to represent the Internet. Hence the name, since cloud computing is defined as Internet-based computing that allows you, via an Internet connection, to access software or data that is stored and operated on someone else's computer systems (see Figure A.1).

Figure A.1 Cloud Computing

Cloud computing relies on shared computer resources, including software and servers, to deliver information and services to you, the end user. In other words, cloud computing is not the strange, new concept that you may believe it to be. Rather, it is a familiar concept—shared computer resources—with a twenty-first century twist made possible by a number of factors, including ever-increasing Internet speeds.

Of course, that definition of cloud computing is rather simplistic, and there is a continuing debate among computing experts regarding the parameters of the concept of cloud computing and the "correct" definition of the term.

Some contend that cloud computing is essentially an extension of the "grid computing" of yesteryear (a local computer cluster which is likened to a grid because it is composed of multiple nodes), while others claim that it is an entirely new phenomenon. Still others describe it as web-based computing, utility computing, or networked computers that function as supercomputers.

But most would agree that cloud computing is a type of technology that offers dramatic improvements in using shared resources at very low prices. In the consumer marketplace, when used as IT services, cloud computing allows a law office to consider the option of replacing its own on-site IT operations with convenient, Internet-based storage and services that can be accessed from any place, at any time of the day or night.

Index

A

ABA Commission on Ethics 20/20,
147–148
Abacus, xxiii
Access
granting, to Gmail accounts, 45–46
offline, to Gmail messages, 65–66
Accounts. *See* Gmail accounts
Accounts Settings tab, 42–43
checking mail for other accounts
option, 43–44
granting access to, 45–47
Send Mail As, 44–45
Administrator's Control Panel, Gmail
actions for when employees leave
firm, 122–125
controlling e-mail attachments,
120–122
managing, 119–122
Advanced Search options, 55–56
Advantages
of Cloud-based Google Apps, xxi–
xxiii
Calendar, 78, 89
Gmail, xx–xxi
Advologix, xxiii
Agenda view, Calendar, printing, 100–101
Aliases, creating, 118
Allison, G. Burgess, 51

B

Backing up information, Google Apps
Accounts and, 141
Boomerang, 135
Browser setting, 32
Burton, Chad, xviii, 2
Business center computers, avoiding,
xxii, 138

All Mail labels, 17
Always Use HTTPS, 32
Ancillary tools, xvii
Appointments, searching for, 97–98. *See
also* Google Calendar
Attachments, e-mail, controlling,
120–122
attachment compliance filters,
112–126
how to attach a file, 26
large limits, xx

C

Calendar. *See* Google Calendar
Calendar Details tab, 104–106
Calendar Labs Tab, 109
Calendar Mobile Setup tab, 108–109

167

Calendar Reminders and Notifications
  tab, 107–108
Calendars Setting tab, sharing Calendar
  using, 104
Call Phone, xvii, 79–80
Cameras, setting up, 71
Canned Responses
  lab option, 39–41
  sending, 52
Chat, xvii, 16. *See also* Google Chat/
  Google Talk
Circles labels, 16
Clio, xxiii
Cloud-based Google Apps, advantages
  of, xxi–xxiii
Cloud computing, defined, 163–165
Code of Conduct, Google, 146
Colors, adding label, 21
Common law duties, of attorneys, 161
Compose message, 2–4
Conduct, Google Code of, 146
Confidentiality, 137–138
  Google Apps and, xviii–xix
Contacts Manager
  about, 57–58
  adding new contacts manually, 58–59
  adding other contacts to contacts,
    59–60
  creating groups of contacts, 60
Conversation View, 9–11
  turned off, 12
Crandall, Marc S., 138, 141, 142, 148,
  150, 151, 159
Create button, creating events with,
  89–91
Create e-mail aliases sub-tab, 118
Custom labels, 13–14
  creating, 18–19
  managing, 19

D

Dashboard, 115. *See also* Google Apps
  for Business Accounts
Deleting
  attachments, 122
  contacts, 59–60
  labels, 20
  lists, 61
  messages, 25
  tasks, 62
Desktop notifications, 32
Domain Name Provider method, 116
Domains, verifying your, 116
Drafts label, 16
Drive, xvii

E

Edit info link, 44
E-mails, controlling attachments to,
  120–122
Employees
  actions for departing, 122–125
  suspending access to accounts of,
    125
Ethics, 137–161
  Google Apps and, xviii–xix
Ethics Opinions, 145–161
Events. *See also* Google Calendar
  adding, to calendar directly from
    Gmail, 27
  creating, by clicking into Calendar,
    93
  creating, with Create button, 89–91
  creating, with Quick Add box, 92
  editing, 95–96
  searching for, 97–98

Events Attachments, 109
External content, 31
  blocking, 32

F

Federal Information Security
  Management Act of 2000 (FISMA),
  138
Filters
  Attachment Compliance, 120–122
  creating, 44, 49–51
  exporting, 52–53
  importing, 53
  practice tips, 51
  settings, 49–52
  sharing, 52
FISMA (Federal Information Security
  Management Act of 2000), 138
Florida Bar Standing Professional Ethics
  Committee: Proposed Advisory
  Opinion 12-3 (2013), 158
Forms, xvii
Forwarding, 30, 45–51

G

GAMMO (Google Apps Migration for
  Microsoft Outlook), 81–84
General tab, 126
Gmail, xvii. *See also* Settings, Gmail
  accessing, 1–2
  adding events to calendar directly
    from, 27
  ancillary tools in, xvii
  attaching files to messages, 5–7
  Call Phone within, 79–80

composing messages, 2–6
Contacts Manager, 57–60
conversation view, 9–11
Inbox view, 9–12
labels, 13–21
making Web interface as default
  method for sending, 5
managing groups of messages in,
  23–25
managing individual messages in,
  25–28
migrating existing e-mail messages
  to, 81–84
offline access to messages, 65j–67
ownership of information and,
  142–144
search and retrieval capability for, xxv
search capabilities, 55–56
spam-filtering and, xxiv
storage space and, xxiv
Tasks Manager, 60–63
turning off conversation view, 11
Gmail accounts
  granting accessing to, 45–47
  sending messages and using other
    e-mail addresses in From line for,
    44–45
  signing up, 116
  suspending employee, 125
Gmail Administrator's Control Panel
  actions for when employees leave
    firm, 122–125
  controlling e-mail attachments,
    120–122
  managing, 119–122
Google Account, xxv
  type appropriate for lawyers, xxvii–
    xxviii
  types of, xxv–xxvii

Google Apps
    confidentiality ethical obligations of
        lawyers and, 145–158
    differences between free and paid,
        158–159
    reasons for using, in law offices, xx
Google Apps accounts
    adding users to, 117–118
    backing up information and, 141
    Create e-mail aliases, 118
    ownership of information and,
        142–144
    setting up, 116–117
    updating Mail Exchanger (MX)
        records, 118–119
Google Apps for Business, xvi
Google Apps for Business Accounts, 115
    adding users, 117–118
    Administrator's Control Panel,
        119–122
    creating, 116
    employee departures and, 122–125
    setting up, 116–117
    signing up for, 116
    updating Mail Exchanger (MX)
        records, 118–119
    verifying and activating, 115
Google Apps for Business with Vault,
    xxvi
Google Apps for Education, xxvi
Google Apps for Government, xxvi
    City of Los Angeles and, 144–145
Google Apps for Non-Profits, xxvi
Google Apps Marketplace, 133–134
    common plug-ins in, examples of,
        135
Google Apps Migration for Microsoft
    Outlook (GAMMO), 81–84

Google Apps suite, xxv
    advantages of cloud-based, xxi–xxv
    confidentiality and, xviii–xix
    defined, xvii–xviii
    ethics and, xviii–xix
    reasons for using, in law offices, xviii,
        xx
    saving money and, xxiii
    security and, xviii–xix
Google Calendar. *See also* Events;
    Settings tab, Google Calendar
    accessing, without Internet
        connection, 111–113
    adding events to, directly from
        Gmail, 27
    adding new events to, 89–93
    Administrator Control Panel,
        125–127
    advantages of, 86–87
    creating multiple, 86
    customizing, 103–109
    editing events already added to,
        95–96
    embedding, in existing Web site, 106
    example of, 87–88
    printing, 99–102
    search and retrieval capability for, xxv
    searching for events and
        appointments in, 97–98
    syncing, with stand-alone products,
        86
Google Calendar Administrator Control
    Panel
    General tab, 126
    Org Settings tab, 125–126
    Resources tab, 126–127
Google Calendar gadget, 41–42
    getting started with, 85–88

Google Chat/Google Talk
about, 69–70
if person is online, 76–77
initiating, 75–76
Off the record, 72–73
reporting statistics back to Google, 72
saving transcripts, 72–73
settings, 70–71
starting, 73–75
text, 75–76
video, 75–76
voice, 75–76
Google Chrome Web Store, 134
common plug-ins in, examples of, 135
Google Code of Conduct, 146
Google Docs
gadget, 39
previews in mail lab option, 42
Google Drive, xvii
Google Gmail. *See* Gmail
Google Hangout, xvii, 70
Google Presentations, xvii
Google Spreadsheets, xvii
Google Vault, 131–132
Grant access to your account option, 45–47

H

Hangout, xvii, 70
Hasbrook, Clayton, xx
HoudiniESQ, xxiii
HTML File Upload Method, 116
HTML Tag Method, 116
HTTPS, Always Use, 32
Hunter, Eric, xix, xxi, 139

I

IMAP Access, 48–49
Important labels, 15–16
Inbox label, 13
Inbox view, 9–12
Information
backing up, 151
common law duties of attorneys to safeguard, 161
ownership of, Gmail and, 142–144
Insert
invitations, 4
links, 4
photos, 4
International Standards Organization (ISO) 27001 certification, 139, 140
Iowa State Bar Ethics Opinion 11-01 (2011), 153

J

Jaffee, Jonathan, 163
Jump to date, 109

K

Keyboard shortcuts, 31
Kovacs, Andrew, 144

L

Labeling, 13
Labels
adding colors, 21
All Mail, 17

Chats, 16
Circles, 16
Custom, 13, 18–19
deleting, 20
Drafts, 16
Important, 15–16
Inbox, 15
managing, 21
Sent Mail, 16
Spam, 17
Starred, 15
System, 13–15, 19
Trash, 17
Labs settings, 36
Canned Responses, 39–41
Google calendar gadgets, 41
Google docs gadget, 41
sample, 37
Undo Send, 38–39
Labs tab, Calendar, 109
Levin, Randi, 144
Los Angeles, City of, use of Google Apps and, 144–145

M

Mail Exchanger (MX) records, updating, 118–119
Maine State Bar Professional Ethics Commission Opinion 194 (2008), 149–150
Marketplace, Google Apps, 133–134
plug-ins, examples of, 135
Massachusetts Bar Association Ethics Opinion 12-03 (2012), 156
Messages, Gmail
composing, 2–6
forwarding, 49

managing groups of, 23–25
managing individual, 25–28
offline access to, 65–67
printing, 26
Microphones, setting up, 71
Mobile Setup tab, Calendar, 108–109
Mute conversation, 11–12
MX (Mail Exchanger) records, updating, 118–119
MyCase, xxiii
My Picture option, 33

N

New Jersey Advisory Committee on Professional Ethics Opinion 701 (2006), 149
New York State Bar Association's Committee on Professional Ethics 820 (2008), 150
New York State Bar Association's Committee on Professional Ethics Opinion 842 (2010), 151–152
North Carolina Bar Association 2011 Formal Ethics Opinion 6 (2011), 154–155

O

Off the record, 69
Offline access
to Calendar, 111–113
to Gmail messages, 65–66
Oregon State Bar Association's Formal Ethics Opinion 2011-188 (2011), 152–153
Org Settings tab, 125–126

Index 173

P

Passwords
> changing user's, 123–125
> practice of sharing, 46

Pennsylvania Bar Association Formal
> Opinion 2011-200 (2011), 155–156

People Widget, 33

Personal level indicator, 35

Plug-ins, examples of, in Marketplace
> and Web Store, 135

POP Download, 47–48

Port, Larry, xxiii

Practice management software,
> integrating with, xxiii

Public computers, avoiding, xxii, 138

Q

Quick Add box, creating events with,
> 92

R

Rapportive, 135

Reminders and Notifications tab,
> Calendar, 107–108

Rename user feature, 124

Resources tab, 126–127

Ries, David G., 140, 161

Rocket Matter, xxiii

S

Safe Harbor Program (European Union),
> 140

Search Calendar box, 97–98

Search Google Messages
> advanced, 56
> simple, 55–56

Security, 137–138
> Google Apps and, xviii–xix

*Security Whitepaper: Google Apps Message
and Collaboration Products,* 146

Send Mail As setting, 44–45

Sent Mail labels, 16

Settings, Gmail, 29–30. *See also* Gmail
> Accounts, 42–43
> browser, 32
> creating contacts for Auto-Complete,
> > 33–34
> desktop notifications, 32
> external content, 31–32
> Filters, 49–53
> forwarding, 47–49
> general, 30–31
> keyboard shortcuts, 31
> Labs, 36–41
> My Picture option, 33
> People Widget, 33
> Personal level indicator, 35
> POP/IMAP, 47–49
> Snippets, 35
> Stars, 35–36
> Vacation Responder, 34–35
> Web Clips, 53–54

Settings tab, Google Calendar. *See also*
> Google Calendar
> Calendar Details, 104–106
> Labs tab, 109
> mobile setup, 108–109
> Reminders and Notifications tab,
> > 107–108
> Share this Calendar tab, 106–107
> sharing calendar, 104
> time zone, 103–104

Share this Calendar tab, 106–107
Shortcuts, keyboard, 31
Simple Search options, 55–56
Sites, xvii
Smart Rescheduler, 109
Snippets, 35
Spam labels, 17
Speakers, setting up, 71
Spellcheck, 4
Starred labels, 15
Stars, 35–36
State Bar of Arizona Ethics Opinion 09-04 (2009), 150–151
State Bar of Arizona Ethics Opinion 05-104 (2005), 148
State Bar of California Standing Committee on Professional Responsibility and Conduct: Formal Opinion 2010-179 (2010), 152
State Bar of California Standing Committee on Professional Responsibility and Conduct: Formal Opinion 2012-184 (2012), 157
Statement on Standards for Attestation Engagements (SSAE) 16 Type II audit, 139
Suspend button, 125
Syncing, xvi, xviii–xix, 48, 67, 86, 113
System labels, 13–15
    managing, 19

T

Tasks Manager, 60–63
Text chat. *See* Google Chat/Google Talk

Time Zone, setting your, 103–104
Time zone link, 91
Transcripts, Google Chat, saving, 72–73
Trash labels, 17
2-step Authentication
    turning on, 128
    turning on enforcement of, 129
2-step Verification Enrollment Report, 128

U

Undo Send labs feature, 38–39

V

Vacation Responder, 34–35, 123
Verification codes, 128
Video chat. *See* Google Chat/Google Talk
Voice Calling, xvii
Voice chat. *See* Google Chat/Google Talk

W

Web Clips setting, 53–54
Web Store, Google Chrome, 134
    plug-ins, examples of, 135

SELECTED BOOKS FROM

The Lawyer's Guide to Microsoft Word 2010
By Ben M. Schorr
Product Code: 5110721 / LPM Price: $41.95 / Regular Price: $69.95

Microsoft® Word is one of the most used applications in the Microsoft® Office suite. This handy reference includes clear explanations, legal-specific descriptions, and time-saving tips for getting the most out of Microsoft Word®—and customizing it for the needs of today's legal professional. Focusing on the tools and features that are essential for lawyers in their everyday practice, this book explains in detail the key components to help make you more effective, more efficient, and more successful.

Google for Lawyers: Essential Search Tips and Productivity Tools
By Carole A. Levitt and Mark E. Rosch
Product Code: 5110704 / LPM Price: $47.95 / Regular Price: $79.95

This book introduces novice Internet searchers to the diverse collection of information locatable through Google. The book discusses the importance of including effective Google searching as part of a lawyer's due diligence, and cites case law that mandates that lawyers should use Google and other resources available on the Internet, where applicable. For intermediate and advanced users, the book unlocks the power of various advanced search strategies and hidden search features they might not be aware of.

LinkedIn in One Hour for Lawyers
By Dennis Kennedy and Allison C. Shields
Product Code: 5110737 / LPM Price: $19.95 / Regular Price: $34.95

Lawyers work in a world of networks, connections, referrals, and recommendations. For many lawyers, the success of these networks determines the success of their practice. LinkedIn®, the premier social networking tool for business, can help you create, nurture, and expand your professional network and gain clients in the process. LinkedIn® in One Hour for Lawyers provides an introduction to this powerful tool in terms that any attorney can understand. In just one hour, you will learn to:

- Set up a LinkedIn account
- Complete your basic profile
- Create a robust, dynamic profile that will attract clients
- Build your connections
- Use search tools to enhance your network
- Maximize your presence with features such as groups, updates, answers, and recommendations
- Monitor your network with ease
- Optimize your settings for privacy concerns
- Use LinkedIn® effectively in the hiring process
- Develop a LinkedIn strategy to grow your legal network

The Electronic Evidence and Discovery Handbook: Forms, Checklists, and Guidelines
By Sharon D. Nelson, Bruce A. Olson, and John W. Simek
Product Code: 5110569 / LPM Price: $99.95 / Regular Price: $129.95

The use of electronic evidence has increased dramatically over the past few years, but many lawyers still struggle with the complexities of electronic discovery. This substantial book provides lawyers with the templates they need to frame their discovery requests and provides helpful advice on what they can subpoena. In addition to the ready-made forms, the authors also supply explanations to bring you up to speed on the electronic discovery field. The accompanying CD-ROM features over 70 forms, including, Motions for Protective Orders, Preservation and Spoliation Documents, Motions to Compel, Electronic Evidence Protocol Agreements, Requests for Production, Internet Services Agreements, and more. Also included is a full electronic evidence case digest with over 300 cases detailed!

Facebook in One Hour for Lawyers
By Dennis Kennedy and Allison C. Shields
Product Code: 5110745 / LPM Price: $24.95 / Regular Price: $39.95

With a few simple steps, lawyers can use Facebook® to market their services, grow their practices, and expand their legal network—all by using the same methods they already use to communicate with friends and family. *Facebook® in One Hour for Lawyers* will show any attorney—from Facebook® novices to advanced users—how to use this powerful tool for both professional and personal purposes.

Blogging in One Hour for Lawyers
By Ernie Svenson
Product Code: 5110744 / LPM Price: $24.95 / Regular Price: $39.95

Until a few years ago, only the largest firms could afford to engage an audience of millions. Now, lawyers in any size firm can reach a global audience at little to no cost—all because of blogs. An effective blog can help you promote your practice, become more "findable" online, and take charge of how you are perceived by clients, journalists and anyone who uses the Internet. Blogging in One Hour for Lawyers will show you how to create, maintain, and improve a legal blog—and gain new business opportunities along the way. In just one hour, you will learn to:

- Set up a blog quickly and easily
- Write blog posts that will attract clients
- Choose from various hosting options like Blogger, TypePad, and WordPress
- Make your blog friendly to search engines, increasing your ranking
- Tweak the design of your blog by adding customized banners and colors
- Easily send notice of your blog posts to Facebook and Twitter
- Monitor your blog's traffic with Google Analytics and other tools
- Avoid ethics problems that may result from having a legal blog

TO ORDER VISIT **WWW.SHOPABA.ORG** OR CALL 1-800-285-2221

SELECTED BOOKS FROM

Virtual Law Practice:
How to Deliver Legal Services Online
By Stephanie L. Kimbro

Product Code: 5110707 / LPM Price: $47.95 / Regular Price: $79.95

The legal market has recently experienced a dramatic shift as lawyers seek out alternative methods of practicing law and providing more affordable legal services. Virtual law practice is revolutionizing the way the public receives legal services and how legal professionals work with clients. If you are interested in this form of practicing law, *Virtual Law Practice* will help you:

- *Responsibly deliver legal services online to* your clients
- Successfully set up and operate a virtual law office
- Establish a virtual law practice online through a secure, client-specific portal
- Manage and market your virtual law practice
- Understand state ethics and advisory opinions
- Find more flexibility and work/life balance in the legal profession

Social Media for Lawyers: The Next Frontier
By Carolyn Elefant and Nicole Black

Product Code: 5110710 / LPM Price: $47.95 / Regular Price: $79.95

The world of legal marketing has changed with the rise of social media sites such as LinkedIn, Twitter, and Facebook. Law firms are seeking their companies attention with tweets, videos, blog posts, pictures, and online content. Social media is fast and delivers news at record pace. This book provides you with a practical, goal-centric approach to using social media in your law practice that will enable you to identify social media platforms and tools that fit your practice and implement them easily, efficiently, and ethically.

iPad Apps in One Hour for Lawyers
By Tom Mighell

Product Code: 5110739 / LPM Price: $19.95 / Regular Price: $34.95

At last count, there were more than 80,000 apps available for the iPad. Finding the best apps often can be an overwhelming, confusing, and frustrating process. iPad Apps in One Hour for Lawyers provides the "best of the best" apps that are essential for any law practice. In just one hour, you will learn about the apps most worthy of your time and attention. This book will describe how to buy, install, and update iPad apps, and help you:

- Find apps to get organized and improve your productivity
- Create, manage, and store documents on your iPad
- Choose the best apps for your law office, including litigation and billing apps
- Find the best news, reading, and reference apps
- Take your iPad on the road with apps for travelers
- Maximize your social networking power
- Have some fun with game and entertainment apps during your relaxation time

Twitter in One Hour for Lawyers
By Jared Correia

Product Code: 5110746 / LPM Price: $24.95 / Regular Price: $39.95

More lawyers than ever before are using Twitter to network with colleagues, attract clients, market their law firms, and even read the news. But to the uninitiated, Twitter's short messages, or tweets, can seem like they are written in a foreign language. Twitter in One Hour for Lawyers will demystify one of the most important social-media platforms of our time and teach you to tweet like an expert. In just one hour, you will learn to:

- Create a Twitter account and set up your profile
- Read tweets and understand Twitter jargon
- Write tweets—and send them at the appropriate time
- Gain an audience—follow and be followed
- Engage with other Twitters users
- Integrate Twitter into your firm's marketing plan
- Cross-post your tweets with other social media platforms like Facebook and LinkedIn
- Understand the relevant ethics, privacy, and security concerns
- Get the greatest possible return on your Twitter investment
- And much more!

The Lawyer's Essential Guide to Writing
By Marie Buckley

Product Code: 5110726 / LPM Price: $47.95 / Regular Price: $79.95

This is a readable, concrete guide to contemporary legal writing. Based on Marie Buckley's years of experience coaching lawyers, this book provides a systematic approach to all forms of written communication, from memoranda and briefs to e-mail and blogs. The book sets forth three principles for powerful writing and shows how to apply those principles to develop a clean and confident style.

iPad in One Hour for Lawyers, Second Edition
By Tom Mighell

Product Code: 5110747 / LPM Price: $24.95 / Regular Price: $39.95

Whether you are a new or a more advanced iPad user, *iPad in One Hour for Lawyers* takes a great deal of the mystery and confusion out of using your iPad. Ideal for lawyers who want to get up to speed swiftly, this book presents the essentials so you don't get bogged down in technical jargon and extraneous features and apps. In just six, short lessons, you'll learn how to:

- Quickly Navigate and Use the iPad User Interface
- Set Up Mail, Calendar, and Contacts
- Create and Use Folders to Multitask and Manage Apps
- Add Files to Your iPad, and Sync Them
- View and Manage Pleadings, Case Law, Contracts, and other Legal Documents
- Use Your iPad to Take Notes and Create Documents
- Use Legal-Specific Apps at Trial or in Doing Research

TO ORDER VISIT **WWW.SHOPABA.ORG** OR CALL 1-800-285-2221

30-DAY RISK-FREE ORDER FORM

Please print or type. To ship UPS, we must have your street address. If you list a P.O. Box, we will ship by U.S. Mail.

Name

Member ID

Firm/Organization

Street Address

City/State/Zip

Area Code/Phone (In case we have a question about your order)

E-mail

Method of Payment:
❏ Check enclosed, payable to American Bar Association
❏ MasterCard   ❏ Visa   ❏ American Express

Card Number   Expiration Date

Signature Required

MAIL THIS FORM TO:
American Bar Association, Publication Orders
P.O. Box 10892, Chicago, IL 60610

ORDER BY PHONE:
24 hours a day, 7 days a week:
Call 1-800-285-2221 to place a credit card order.
We accept Visa, MasterCard, and American Express.

EMAIL ORDERS: orders@americanbar.org
FAX: 1-312-988-5568

VISIT OUR WEB SITE: www.ShopABA.org
Allow 7-10 days for regular UPS delivery. Need it sooner? Ask about our overnight delivery options. Call the ABA Service Center at 1-800-285-2221 for more information.

GUARANTEE:
If–for any reason–you are not satisfied with your purchase, you may return it within 30 days of receipt for a refund of the price of the book(s). No questions asked.

Thank You For Your Order.

Join the ABA Law Practice Management Section today and receive a substantial discount on Section publications!

Product Code:	Description:	Quantity:	Price:	Total Price:
				$
				$
				$
				$
				$

Subtotal	$
*Tax:	$
**Shipping/Handling:	$
Yes, I am an ABA member and would like to join the Law Practice Management Section today! (Add $50.00)	$
Total:	$

**Shipping/Handling:
$0.00 to $9.99	add $0.00
$10.00 to $49.99	add $5.95
$50.00 to $99.99	add $7.95
$100.00 to $199.99	add $9.95
$200.00 to $499.99	add $12.95

*Tax:
IL residents add 9.75%
DC residents add 6%

TO ORDER VISIT **WWW.SHOPABA.ORG** OR CALL 1-800-285-2221

ABA WEBSTORE: WWW.SHOPABA.ORG

ITUNES: WWW.APPLE.COM/ITUNES

LAW PRACTICE MANAGEMENT
RESOURCES FOR THE DIGITAL AGE

LPM e-books are now available to read on your iPad, smartphone, or favorite e-reader! To download the **latest releases** in EPUB or Apple format, visit the ABA Webstore or iTunes today. LPM's digital library is expanding quickly, so check back often for new e-book availability. Purchase LPM e-books today and be only **one click away** from the resources your law practice needs.

FOLLOW LPM!

Stay current with the latest news about LPM Books, including discount offers, free excerpts, author interviews, and more.

- t LPM Books Blog: http://lpmbooks.tumblr.com/
- t @LawPracticeTips
- f http://www.facebook.com/LawPracticeTips
- in ABA Law Practice Management Section Group